HEAL

Heal

by Mynavati

ISBN : 81-86847-07-3

Publishers : Tiger Moon Productions/Cosmic Power Press
email : cosmicpowerpress@yahoo.co.in

Price : £10.99

I dedicate this book to God,
to God in Form, the Poorna Avatar—
my Beloved Guru, Bhagavan Sri Sathya Sai Baba,
to all the teachers, guides and helpers, God has given to me,
and
to all of God's creation
on the Quest
of
Healing towards Wholeness

Guru Poornima Eve, 23rd July 2002

Disclaimer

The author and publishers are not responsible for any injury to any person attempting to use the practices and methods described in this book.

The reader is requested to take responsibility for his or her mental and physical health and balance. If in doubt as to whether or not you can safely use the practices and methods described in this book, please consult with a professional.

If you have a history of mental illness, alcohol or drug-abuse, or if you are experiencing depression, suicidal tendencies, sleeplessness or nervous exhaustion, please seek professional and ongoing guidance before attempting any continuous spiritual practices and methods.

I Believe

There is a spark of Divinity within everyone and everything,
animate and inanimate,
and within every being in the Universe
and Beyond.

I believe
the spark within us and within everyone and everything
is God.

I believe that God is Formless and is Everywhere
but that at any point God chooses
you can see God in Form.

I believe that there is such a thing as Wholeness.

I believe that there is such a thing as Healing.

I believe that there is such thing as Pure Love.

I believe that in saying any of these words,
we are also talking of God, the Healer,
and becoming Whole.

I believe that there is continuing Life after Death.

I believe in Reincarnation.

I believe in the Law of Cause and Effect, in Karma.

I believe in Freedom
from the idea of the Cycle of Birth and Death.

I believe that there is no Death.

I believe that there is no Birth.

I believe that God and we are One.

I believe in Goodness.

I believe that everything and everyone at every time
is, according to Divine Will and Play,
in a state of Perfection.

I believe that we began a journey of discovery long ago
and though we never leave Home,
our True Self,
where we are completely immersed in Love,
we spend many lifetimes following the Circular Path
back to the Start,
back to Ourselves.

I believe in Miracles.

I believe in the Power of Prayer.

I believe that all is as it should be.

Mynavati

Forward

There was a famous sculptor in Italy known as Michaelangelo. A friend of his found him one day chiselling a big piece of rock. The friend told him: "Why are you working so hard with this rock? Why don't you go home and take some rest?" Michaelangelo replied: "I am trying to release the Divine that is in the rock. I wish to bring out of this lifeless stone the Living Divinity that is embodied in it.

If that sculptor could create, out of an inanimate piece of stone, a living Image of God, cannot human beings vibrant with life manifest the living Divinity that resides in them?

Baghawan Sri Sathya Sai Baba
(Indian Avatar living in the township of
Prashanti Nilayam, Andhra Pradesh)

You may feel that you need to be healed. Perhaps you want to be a *healer*. Perhaps you are interested in both. Actually, it is impossible to be one without the other. Maybe you know nothing about healing, but something drew you to the book, perhaps the cover or the word *Heal* itself. We do not always have to know why we do something. Yet, usually, everything reveals itself as time unfolds.

We all need healing and we are all healers. This is true whether we identify with the terms or not. The journey to Wholeness, to Divinity, is ongoing and unfolding, that is, until we find that we are finally free and at one with the Divine within us, at one with God. Then there is Wholeness. A life of ignorance is a life full of suffering. When we realise this, we have the readiness to dive deeper into our beings, and to **HEAL**. When we do this we become willing participants in our learning and growing, and so, our reaction to our difficulties becomes less contracted. We begin to face our difficulties with more openness of heart and wisdom. Rather than push them away, we transform our difficulties and ourselves by facing them. We face ourselves and begin to accept and have compassion for ourselves. We learn how to be vigilant, have discrimination and mindfulness. We learn how to witness others and ourselves without judgement. We learn how to *practice* to be Whole, until our false self, the illusion that is less than our Wholeness and which we identify with, drops away.

We all want to **HEAL**, but we are often unaware of the fullness of the healing that we can have. In this search, many people have become identified as healers or as patients. Some as both! Some people simply feel love for others and for the earth and, through this love, healing rays from their spiritual heart spread out in a natural and unconsciously beautiful way. Occasionally some go further in their ideals and are on a mission and want to save the world, but often they are yet to save themselves.

There are those of you, I know, who have been healing yourselves or others for some time now, but have grown tired and feel drained and disillusioned. What went wrong?

Whatever your role, stage or setting you are on a wonderful path and that this journey is leading you towards Home. You can only move towards the Self, your Divine Self. There is no one, no place and nothing else other than You. Your journey then can only end in the pure joy of finally coming Home. Every road leads to this joy regardless of its name, for there is only one destination. But this book is for those who are exploring the way. This book is to help you on your quest.

Some ways of healing are mentioned here and looked at, but the material does not belong to any particular school or form of healing. Healing *is*. The way you choose to do it will be your particular preference. It is not the method that is necessarily important, but the attitude, the understanding and the degree of honesty that accompanies it. On any path there are numerous pitfalls, bumps, detours and bridges. Along the way you will also encounter illusion, delusion and ego-inflation. This book is to help you with some of these.

There are some exercises and meditations in the chapters that you can use when you feel the need to. Every spiritual difficulty we have has an antidote. There are some you will feel attracted to and you may not feel attracted to others. All the remedies are for both self-exploration and when appropriate, for working with others.

When reference is made to self-healing, this can also be used for the healing of others. When reference is made to the healing of others, this can also be used for self-healing. Truly, there is only "one" who is being healed and who is the healer. *We* are *One.*

On your foundation, the roots of your growth place everything in the context of this impermanent and ever-changing reality. You will not always feel happy. Despair and disillusionment are part of your journey. Actually, these feelings are an indication that you are doing well and that whatever you are doing is working. Remember at these times that it is only your ego that can have these feelings. Your True Self is always in bliss. Your aim is to destroy the ego's power and illusion over you. You can in fact rejoice when your ego feels despair for it means that it is weakening. Remember too, that you do not have to take it all too seriously! It is your birthright to also feel the joy and the fun of the exploration you are now undertaking.

Mynavati

Table of Contents

Introduction 3

Part I

Heal, Chapter 1 5
Commitment and Persistence 5
Perspective 8

Self-Love, Chapter 2 17
Respect and Serve Others 30

Anger, Chapter 3 34

Fear, Chapter 4 43

Trust, Chapter 5 51
Papaji's Story 54

Gratitude, Chapter 6 59

Compassion, Chapter 7 69

Surrender, Chapter 8 79
The Surrender of the Bullfrog 83

Death, Chapter 9 87

Part II

Some Practical Things to Do
Healing and Wholeness, Chapter 10 101
The Dirty Old Coat 102

The Dream, Chapter 11 107
Dreamwork 109
Dream Teachings 118

Using a Journal, Chapter 12 122
Expressing Your Feelings by Letter 131

Intuition and Symbols, Chapter 13 134
Symptoms, Causes and Effects 137
Intuitive Knowing and Symbols 140
Can I Trust This or Not? 143
Messages for Others 146
Symbol Synchronicity 149

Prayer and Meditation in Our Healing Towards Wholeness, Chapter 14 154
Prayer as an Offering of Love to Love 158
Meditation and Healing Towards Wholeness 159

Self-Healing, Chapter 15 164

Honouring Your Energy, Chapter 16 174

Honouring Time and Space, Chapter 17 182
The Sacredness of the Cycles of Time 185
Your Sacred Space 191
The Mayan Crystal Skull 193

Honouring Your Quest, Chapter 18 198
Our Old Habits 206

Credits 216

Suggested Reading 218

Part I

Introduction

When I meditated on the word *Heal,* I came to the awareness that a word, just like a mantra, can have power. The word itself can transmit a sacred message to you. This is the message I received from the word **Heal**:

This is an Initiation into healing,
which begins
with the Transmission
of the word HEAL.

The meaning of HEAL *cannot*
be defined in words.
It can only be experienced and felt.
The Transmission comes from the energy of the word itself.
It begins when you say the word HEAL *internally*
or aloud,
at the same time connecting
to the Divine flow within your heart and all around.

You will find that inherent in the word
is its ability to ignite and transform.
Feel its Love in your heart.
Feel HEAL *now.*
The word HEAL *will take you on a journey of transformation,*
towards hope, truth, love and peace.
And, like you, the word is multidimensional.
It works on every level of your being.
Like you, it has no beginning and no end.

HEAL *is something to be felt and explored.*
It reveals to us our story of Living and Dying and being Reborn.

It tells us about our poignant journey of experience
in the beautiful setting of this world.

You were placed in this world to grow
towards loving yourself,
and others in fullness.
You were placed in this world to explore the truth, of
Who you really are,
to go beyond the limitations of your body, time and space,
beyond that, which you can merely feel, hear or see.

You were born in this world to discover your Divinity,
placed on this earth to know that you are Divine.
You are in this world to HEAL *yourself*
*and to let this **LOVE** heal the world.*
Healing means Wholeness.
Wholeness means Love.
Love means God

HEAL

HEAL

1

Divers search in the ocean for pearls; they don't find them every time. They may have to dive twenty or thirty times in the deep sea to get them—and even then they don't always succeed. Sometimes they may not find certain pearls for years, although the pearls are there. The diver is doing his duty, but he is not getting a reward. Each of us must likewise make repeated efforts in our own life. Always make an effort. But there should be sincerity in it.

Swami Rama—*Inspired Thoughts of Swami Rama*

Commitment and Persistence

To enter the ray of healing you need only connect to the word HEAL and believe it as real. You only need to know that you can HEAL.

To HEAL you need only a commitment to finding out the truth of yourself. To find yourself even interested in the word HEAL, means that you are ready for the next step. Combine your interest with sincerity and persistence and you will reap the harvest of your Divine inheritance and birthright. You will find Wholeness.

With some people one step may seem to take years. With others it may appear to happen in an instant. To many it can feel like a long process, a journey that takes them on seeming dummy runs, false starts and blocked roadways.

With some travellers, healing means of the body, spirit, or mind. With others, it is a search for the *Self.* Some wish to find healing through the desire for a better life and others as their vehicle of transformation. Some people know healing towards Wholeness as their final Truth, Liberation and Freedom. No matter what you believe in or think that healing is, you are on the journey whether you wish to be or not and its destination is your Wholeness. No one will miss out on this terminus. You may get off at a prior stop for a little sojourn. This particular rest from your true journey may take a whole life, lifetimes even, but eventually, your time in any locality will end and you will need to get back on the bus. You will reach the final destination eventually. It is all a question of time and timing and Divine Will. So, you can relax knowing that you will get there and in the meantime you can enjoy the view.

Final Destination

Once there was an old woman that got a ticket for a bus journey. But, during the trip she could not relax. She was so worried that she might miss her stop, that she might pass it, that she became increasingly agitated as the bus drove onwards. The bus passed through some really beautiful scenery: lakes, mountains, winding roads with views of stunning countryside.

Although the old woman had a window seat, she could not enjoy anything of the view. The journey took a long time and the bus even made stops for people to walk about and have a picnic. But the old woman was so anxious that the bus might go away without her that she did not get off. In fact, each time the bus stopped she almost had a nervous breakdown with fear and worry in case this was her stop and she would miss it.

Eventually, the bus came to the final stop of the terminus and the driver told her that she had arrived. By now, she had become so anxious and fearful that she did not believe him. She asked the driver how he knew that it was really her stop. He replied, "Because, Ma'am, your ticket was for the terminus, and now the journey is over."

Our lives are like this. Every body we occupy has a journey and a terminus, and every ego we have also has a terminus. We all have a final destination. We can journey towards this *stop* with anxiety and fear, or we can relax and enjoy the view. It is up to us.

When you think about the word HEAL forget judgements and comparisons. Remember that everything is of value. Every mistake you have made has been a gift. Every false start has been a boon. Every dummy run has been a strengthening lesson. Trust in the wisdom of blocked roadways and blind alleyways. They have been part of your historic game. You have needed them in order to learn the rules. Trust in perfect timing. You cannot receive anything until you are ready. When it is the right time you are ready. At the right time nothing can stop your healing.

With the word **HEAL** think of your, everyone's and everything's perfection in time and place. Remember, as everything and everyone is in perfection so is your disharmony, disease, despair perfect for you at this time.

As you **HEAL**, have compassion for yourself and everything and everyone. Perfection does not necessarily mean being or feeling comfortable. Perfection does not necessarily mean peace. Pain can be perfect and perfection is often painful. Remember that everyone feels all that you experience. No one is exempt. We are all in this big soup pot of life together, and we are all being Divinely cooked. We are all becoming *Prasad* (Divine Food) for God. As human beings we need love, affection, tenderness, companionship, and devotion. We need to be aware that we are vulnerable. Just as a baby cannot survive on its own and needs its mother, we need each other. And we all need each other to help one another to fulfil our destinies.

The Dalai Lama says of Affection and Compassion:

The basic aim of my explanation is to show that by nature we are compassionate, that compassion is something very necessary and something, which we can develop. It is important to know the exact meaning of compassion. The Buddhist interpretation is that genuine compassion is based on a clear acceptance of recognition that others, like oneself, want happiness and have the right to overcome suffering. On that basis one develops some kind of concern about the welfare of others, irrespective of their attitude to oneself. That is compassion.

The Dalai Lama's Book of Wisdom

What is helpful for us to be aware of is that, in our compassion and affection for one another, we can at any time fall into the snare of attachment. Attachment is affection and compassion gone wrong! When we become attached, we cease to be able to care about others except in relation to ourselves. With attachment, our concern for others is really to have them meet our needs. If their needs comply with ours, there can be a kind of harmony, but this a rare event. Knowing this, and that we are each engaged in a constant struggle between compassion, affection, and its opposite, attachment:

Remember

that you are journeying in a split and illusory world,
that you and all the parts of you which seem to be other people,
other things in this mirage
are all subject to suffering,
so, be soft and gentle with you and others.

Remember
to enjoy what you are given in this garden of
exploration and wonderment,
and fully participate in what can be this beautiful worldly play
of yours and your playmates'
Healing towards Wholeness.

HEAL

Perspective

In our healing adventure we need to remember that we are multidimensional beings. We therefore need to be fed on all levels of our being. That is the emotional, mental and spiritual levels as well as the physical level. It makes complete sense to consider all. Each nourishes the other. All nourish us. One can find an ***entry point*** to our healing by using any one of them as a doorway for going deeper, and each will affect the others. For example, bringing more energy to one level will ultimately have a kick-on effect to the rest. To keep in mind, however, that because of their interdependence, all our levels require help, is to be more consciously aware of their healing and to have a more Whole perspective. This makes for deeper and more extensive transformation.

Susan's Entry Point

Susan had heart palpitations for some time. She had many medical tests done. But the results showed that there were no medical or physiological reasons for the palpitations. This indicated to me that the trouble was possibly emotionally based. ***(Emotional Level)***

These palpitations affected her sleeping pattern, and as a result she became stressed and tired. ***(Physical Level)***

She had anxiety, but she did not know why. ***(Mental Level)***

She also felt scared by the palpitations themselves. What's more, Susan was still recovering from the loss of her husband who died of cancer six months previously. ***(Emotional Level)***

Her husband Ron had been ill for many months, and she nursed him throughout his illness. When she first came to see me, her life force was low. ***(Etheric Level)***

Using clairvoyance, I could see in her energy field, in the Heart Chakra, that the loss of Ron had triggered an even older grief. ***(Astral Body Level and Heart Chakra Level)***

I could identify the shock of her husband's illness and death in her Heart Chakra, because I saw a discoloration in the energy field that looked as recent as a few months ago. Over the years, I have come to recognise this discoloration as being connected with grief and shock. But there was also another radiating and fiery mass underneath this discoloration.

When we talked about what I saw, Susan was able to connect to her deep-rooted fear of being alone, of everyone leaving her. She said that this fear had been with her for as long as she could remember. Her husband's death had finally fulfilled this fear, and she now felt totally isolated, alone and abandoned. ***(Astral Body Level)***

I realised that Susan's desolation was a result of her split from God. This split had perhaps perpetuated itself through many life times. ***(Karmic Level)***

I asked her how she felt about God. She said that she believed that God was punishing her and did not love her. ***(Spiritual Level)***

I decided that the best **point of entry** *for Susan's healing were the feelings she had about God. In my opinion, this was the most fundamental level of her grief, and as she had been able to identify it, we could continue to make her negative spiritual beliefs more conscious so that she could be more connected to them. To feel is to* HEAL.

While she was in my care, Susan spent some weeks writing letters to God, and telling God her heart-rending story, her fears and how she felt alienated from everything and everyone. She was able to tell God how she thought she was being punished, especially through the death of her husband who had been the only person she felt really loved her.

Ultimately, we composed an affirmation for Susan that she said throughout the day:

I affirm
that I am eternally loved, cherished and held by God,
and that this love radiates through my entire life
in everything I do
and in every relationship I have.

Susan also poured out her feelings to her dead husband through the writing of unsent letters to him. In this way she was able to say all the things she needed to say to him, even though he was physically not with her anymore. ***To feel is to*** **HEAL.**

Within a couple of weeks, her heart palpitations lessened and finally stopped. She experienced increasing joy and a feeling of oneness with the world and with the Divine. Her life force increased from the balancing of her ***Spiritual, Karmic, Astral Body, Emotional, Mental, Etheric*** *and Physical Levels. She now had increased energy radiating through her. She literally shone.*

So, you see, the palpitations came as a blessing and enabled Susan to deeply HEAL. *I encouraged her not to stop where she was, but to continue daily, the excersises I had prescribed. In order to achieve more Wholeness, I asked her keep the* ***entry point*** *of her* ***Levels*** *opened by contemplating, meditating and praying in the way she had begun for at least an hour a day for the rest of her life.*

Usually the last manifestations of *dis-ease* are physical symptoms. Normally, this is the only area that is considered by allopathic medicine. But in most cases, some *un-ease* was happening for some time before the person gets to the point of manifesting physical symptoms—as with Susan. If her palpitations, anxiety, stress, low life-force field had continued she would have become, I am sure, chronically and perhaps terminally ill. So, if one merely tries to heal physical symptoms, it is generally not enough. Alleviation might happen for a time, but that is all. Within a relatively short period, the initial imbalance, which remains and underlies the physical symptoms, will continue and the same or more serious symptoms will come again.

Somewhere along the line, not only have we split healing and health from the idea of Wholeness on all levels of our being, but we have also split this sense of Wholeness from its Source. What this fundamentally means is that we have split ourselves from God !

We are inclined to look at healing as something that can be *done* physically and externally, rather than the *perfect* outcome of our more complete spiritual journey. This is reflected in the way *Healing* is often being taught nowadays—as a mere hands-on technique without any inclusion of God, Divinity or Spirituality. People are being encouraged to **HEAL** others without even thinking of their own possible *splits.* In fact, the more the technique is said to be scientific and less spiritually oriented the more popular, expensive and acceptable it usually is! Likewise the more gimmicky, glamorous, glitzy and expensive, the more popular it is. The word Love is used a lot, but is rarely expressed.

Somehow, we have learned how to pay a kind of gratuitous lip service to our True Beings. This lip service is not sincere. It is a con. We talk of Light and Love and have lots of hugging at workshops, but the Spirituality, if present at all, is often forced and not authentic. Perhaps we do this because we have disconnected from our true primordial consciousness—our ability to connect with and honour the Divine in all aspects of life. Primitive peoples, without any New Age certificates, had the Intelligence to revere God. That same God is in us and we are only fooling and cheating ourselves when we make Spirituality a certificate-based exercise without authentic Divinity.

Usually it is only when we find ourselves in crisis that we are compelled to be aware of our true needs. We may then become interested in spirituality or meditation or to have some kind of healing therapy. But our emphasis is on how quickly we can get *through these* and feel good enough to *get on with life,* as before—actually, back to the very life that was our predicament and disease, rather than **HEAL** towards Wholeness! We go back to the way of living that led to our fragmentation.

When you reach a point of crisis, rather than be frightened or feel a victim, have gratitude, for you are being blessed. (Remember Susan.) Rather than look for a quick fix, some super therapy glue to stick you together, see this turning point *not* as a disaster, but as a push to help you on your way to fulfilling your self as a human being—that is, finding out who you really are. A crisis is your launching pad for a potential whole new way of being!

In our splitting from Divinity, we have also become disconnected from an awareness of responsibility for our own healing. We usually look for easy and quick solutions from others. We feel that we need someone else to do it for us. It is understandable that we feel we need this. We have long lost confidence in ourselves as living embodiments of Divinity. We feel helpless and victimised. Also, we live in very material worlds. Everything, including us, is very short-lived. We are conditioned for instant satisfaction of our desires, and we are trapped with our feelings of needing a quick lift. Our happiness and satisfaction are now based on the speed with which we can acquire something. We have forgotten who we are. It is sad, is it not?

If a Divine Oracle told you that your journey towards total healing and Wholeness was going to take another 25,000 lifetimes, I doubt you would feel too happy about it. The idea that there may not be a quick fix fills us with panic and horror. And if these quick cures exist, why not take them, you may ask? There is nothing wrong in taking the fix if we know that it is a tonic and a help to our system and that it is not the permanent cure. We need to use the gift of our discrimination and ask ourselves if this is the deepest healing we can have, or is it a helping hand towards achieving it?

I have a hunch, though, and I am sure that you will too, if you think about it, that by the time you get to even know of the words *Healing* and *Spirituality* and are quite interested in them, you are actually well on the way home.

You may still have a few more lives to live with an ego, but it will hopefully not be another 25,000. No one can guarantee this, of course. Only God knows, and God has the final say! But, at least when you reach towards increasing Wholeness, life itself gets better and better. Increasing conscious awareness of Self-Love, Anger, Fear, Trust, Gratitude, Compassion, Surrender, Death and Happiness are just some of the benefits we receive, and this allows us to be more at peace.

A shift in perspective can work miracles. You see, it does not really matter who is doing the healing with whom. You may need healing interaction and input from many others, but what is important is that you take the responsibility for your own healing, regardless. Let us imagine that you know that you have a job, and this is to **HEAL** (Yourself). The healing is not just for your surface abrasions, but for your deepest wound—which is everybody's wound—the split from Wholeness.

You are the Manager, and there is a Divine Managing Director looking after you. This Director is really God, your Divine Self. God will not sack you, regardless of how inept you appear to be at times, because you are God's beloved child. The help you receive from others is an aid to your project. Your project is *Wholeness.* The other people involved in your job are not your superiors. They are your helpers. Your superior's name is Divine Intelligence. You are the boss of your project, with Divine Supervision.

If you **HEAL** from this perspective you will know that what you are experiencing is an aid to the *real wound.* Likewise, you will not sabotage your duty to your Self, to your ongoing and deepening awareness. Your process of healing will not stop at the first initial improvement. This perspective is very different, for example, than the one where someone is ill or having difficulty in his/her life and seeks out help from others, because the individual is helpless and feels like a victim. A typical scenario of the wrong perspective is:

John's Story

John was feeling tired and stressed. He wanted to feel better for his work and have more energy for his marriage and family. He had no idea how to help himself and he found support from a couple of therapists. One was a body worker and the other was a clinical psychologist. The helpers did their best. John did his best. There was an improvement. John had a feeling of being cured. He re-entered life as before with renewed energy. Suddenly he was able to do what he wanted.

A few months later, however, John found himself feeling tired and helpless again. He felt like a victim. Unfortunately, he needed help again. He sought out other professionals. He again benefited and re-entered his life as before. A few months later, he was again tired and stressed and felt even more helpless and definitely poorer.

Does this sound familiar? Has this happened to you, or to someone you know? The cycle goes on… Disillusionment eventually comes. Sometimes people will experience chronic depression, for there seems to be no way out—no real help or healing, no real chance. But to think this way is to look for crumbs, to be a beggar, rather than realising that you are Divine royalty.

If you think like a beggar rather than the King/Queen you are, it is because you have forgotten that the entire purpose of your life, of every event, of every action is to lead you towards Wholeness—to **HEAL**. What you have done instead is get caught up in the events themselves, thinking that they are essential to your Wholeness. You have split them from their real meaning and purpose and have become lost in them.

If John had realised that his lack of energy might be a sign that he needed to explore himself more, he would not have stopped at the first sign of improvement, or the second. If he thought that having more energy for his work, family etc., was a good thing but not *the* most important thing of his life, his perspective would have helped him. If he had realised that going to therapy was only part of the process toward Wholeness, and that connecting with his Divine Self was the goal, he could have continued—and kept the ***point of entry*** open.

John's story is relevant for those who, at any point in time, give and receive healing, for those who are identified with being *healers*, and for those who see themselves as *patients*. Remember that when you are the giver, in essence, you are no different from the receiver. You are also on the same path towards healing and Wholeness. You are not better off than those you are trying to help are. Everything is relative in the temporary world you find yourself in, and just as you can be of help to some people, there are others more able to help you.

Even if another person's situation seems horrendous to you, forget the sympathy, for to God *your* situation and everybody else's is pretty awful! Sympathy will merely get in the way of any constructive and true interaction between you and others and will tend to make you *superior acting* and egotistic. Rather than sympathy, try having compassion for everyone.

Remember that we are all in the same boat on a choppy, tumultuous sea of changing waves and tides and currents, and we are holding on tightly for dear life. This is the reality. We all need to pray for guidance, help and courage, and *know* that we are being lovingly held by Divine Arms that will get us to shore.

When it is your role to help, remind yourself, before you try to help anyone, that you are not the boss! You are only the boss of yourself. With another, you are merely a helper. The innate Intelligence (the Divinity) of the person you are helping knows what It needs at any point in time and will take what is required, subject to Divine Will.

Offer your actions to Divine Will, and for the good of all concerned. Hand yourself and the healing over to this Divine Intelligence and let It do Its wonderful work. In this way you will remain detached from outcomes—very necessary when giving healing, and you will not become disillusioned when things do not work out as you want or hope.

Do the same when you are trying to help yourself. Do your very best for the *all of you concerned*, but at the same time, hand yourself over to Divine Intelligence and Will and relax in the knowing that you are held, guided and that you will reach the terminus whether you enjoy the journey or not...

Self-Love

2

Let one raise the Self by the Self
and not let the Self within become weak;
The Self is,
indeed, the Self's only friend,
but the Self is also its own enemy

Bhagavad Gita— VI-5

As long as you feel that you are a separate entity from That which is Wholeness you will be subject to the vagaries of relative love. While you are travelling towards your Completeness, you can at least understand that you will be a victim of love's play and you can endeavour to love more and more fully and with purity, until you know that you are Love Itself.

You cannot fully love; you cannot love anyone until you love yourself totally and completely. Until you do this, you will have a dependence on others, on external praise and affirmation. You will feel high when you are seemingly appreciated, and you will feel low when you are neglected or negated. This dependence can make you feel on top of the world, but when the topple comes it can make you feel suicidal. Do you really want to continue on this seesaw?

The truth is that you and everyone in this world will be praised, ridiculed, loved, hated, liked and despised at some time by anyone. But what has this really got to do with you?

The reality is that if you take 100 people and ask them for their opinion of you, you will get 100 different opinions about you, good and bad, which has nothing much to do with you at all, but which will have a lot to say about them. Are you going to continue to live out your precious human life subject to the conditioned and neurotic thoughts of others? Are you going to base your happiness on how one person's mind projects on you? Are you going to be fleetingly happy or sad because of someone else's projected, distorted view of you?

For One Moment

make believe that there are no opinions,
judgements or attitudes
anywhere in the world about you.

For just one moment, make believe that your parents,
your teachers, your friends, your peers, your enemies
hold no attitudes about you.

For at Least One Moment

love yourself.
Allow love for yourself to pour out
from your heart to your entire being,
to every little and precious part of you.
Let this moment
become another moment
and then another moment
until you really do feel
completely and utterly
loved.

HEAL

The truth is that at a certain stage, you cannot judge yourself anymore as you continue towards Wholeness. ***Self-judgement and healing do not go together.*** There are times in our lives when we can do this from morning until night and the only time we stop is when we are judging others. But with an increasing awareness of love, you will not be able to hold onto past or present feelings of self-disgust, self-hatred, self-dislike and self-torment.

Believe it or not, your life is already perfect and always has been. You may not know this consciously, or even wish to believe this. But the truth is, in your perfect life; you have received and undergone the most appropriate personal experiences to help you to grow spiritually. That is it! What is there to judge? How can you feel bad about what you have ever done? Who was it that did the act or had the thought? Who wrote the script?

Sri Sathya Sai Baba says:

Whatever you do, wherever you are placed, believe that God has put you there for that work.

It is easy to look back and say that one should not have done this or done that, but could you really have done it any other way? And if it had never happened what would you know now? If you had never made a mistake, how egotistic would you be now? If you had never hurt anyone or been hurt what would you know of such things?

And, if it is pointless to judge yourself, then how can you judge another? If you can no longer punish yourself, how can you continue to justify wanting to punish another? With the strength and power of your own love, forgive yourself, and with the resultant loving softness you find within you, forgive others. This is one of the hardest movements of our heart. It stretches the heart open and you cannot avoid the resultant ego-pain. But the agony is worth it and is short lived. The joy you feel at the slightest opening of the heart is like the accumulated bliss of a hundred thousand years of ego-satisfaction and self-righteousness.

This opening of the being is the reward and is the yearning.
To deny this Truth is the real suffering and pain.

Try to remember a situation where you felt hurt by someone's actions or words, but you stretched your heart to care to forgive them, to feel for them in their ignorance and their own hurt, and you tried to see life from their point of view rather than your own. Did you not feel good? Do you remember feeling a rush of warmth pervade your being? Did you feel here a sense of opening rather than a contraction?

Jesus said at His time of transition, *Forgive them father, for they know not what they do.* He knew that the people murdering Him thought that they were right. He knew that they could do nothing else than what they did. He knew also their actions provided the means for His Resurrection. Jesus, in His Divinity and Godliness, saw the whole picture. But from the tunnel vision of our ego eyes we can only see a limited view. From our ego eyes, any limitations placed upon us, any reprimands or, even the destruction of our desires is viewed by us as evil.

How can we ever know if what others or we do is right or wrong? There is no right or wrong seen through the eyes of Divine Love. Criminals and saints, carry the same Divine Spark. God loves everybody equally all of the time. But, as long as we are in this relative world, there is right action, which is the action your Conscience directs you towards. And this is always perfect in its timing and placement.

Sai Baba says:

Whatever we speak should come out of the heart. We should speak with all love. Whatever you speak with love is bound to be the truth. When there is no love there is falsehood. We have to take truth as the basis in all pursuits. It is not that easy. We have to practice.

Our conscience is the direct emissary of our love. Our love is the emissary of our conscience. They are the vehicles of our Truth.

For One Moment

just make believe
that you hold no opinions,
judgements,
attitudes,
about anyone,
or anything,
anywhere in the world.

For just one moment,
make believe
that you have never
held an attitude,
opinion or judgement
about anyone
or anything
or any place.

HEAL

There is no one in this relative world but particles of you. The world is holographic, a Divine projection, created by you, of you and for you. You are the projectionist, the screen, and the viewer. Everything is just an aspect of the One. You are the *One*. To know what the world is like, what others are like, why he did this, why she did that, to know anything, turn and look towards yourself. Get to know yourself. Everything is contained in you. Everything *out there* is within you. God is within you and you are within God.

Change you, and you change the world!

Earth scientist, author and lecturer, Gregg Braden says of our Oneness:

You and I are holographic in nature. We are cells of a body that encompass our whole. Your parents are part of the body, as are your friends, your husband or wife, your children. Our lives mirror patterns of experience embedded within patterns of experience, embedded within patterns of experience. Each pattern is whole and complete unto itself. Each pattern provides a vital key to a much larger whole….

This is the nature of the hologram. Each cell functions within its own space while, knowingly or not, is in service to the entire body. It does not take many individuals to anchor a new seed of thinking, feeling or emotion into present patterns of our whole. By becoming the desired outcome, a relatively few individuals may introduce change regardless of how long the old patterns have existed.

Walking Between Two Worlds, The Science of Compassion

Regarding love relationships—as long as you identify with being separate, split from the Whole, you will keep chasing the You *out there*, to acknowledge you. You plead with the You *out there* to look at you and to honour you and to love you, but you do not honour yourself. You continually abandon yourself. You continually hide from yourself. If you look at anyone or anything outside of yourself, know that you are looking at you. Know that however you are will be reflected back to you.

If you do not like what you see,
know that you are looking at a hidden, shadowy part
of yourself.

This shadowy part is made up of aspects of you that you have buried because sometime, somewhere, some lifetime you judged them as unacceptable or, they are aspects of yourself that are longing to be expressed. In fact, sometimes you do not know what they are until the manifest, sometimes quite surprisingly. For example, I am sure you know at least one person who shocked family and friends by suddenly *coming out of the closet.*

You can become more conscious of your shadowy part and express it appropriately, rather than inappropriately. For example, if you find yourself detesting liars, try to go within and really ask yourself why. Do you think it is because they escape responsibility, or because they get away with something? Do you think that they get something you don't?

Maybe you would like to tell a lie and be able to avoid pressure sometimes and get something too for nothing. But, your honesty cannot allow you to do this. So, look at how you can look after yourself appropriately and ease your burden. How can you take the pressure off yourself without lying?

For a start, what about making life easier for yourself—by not being afraid to admit your needs to others? On one level the liar tries to take care of him/her self first and this might be what you need to do. Put yourself first but be honest. Do not be frightened to let people know that you doing this.

Whatever is in your shadowy part that does not get appropriately expressed will remain dormant eating away at you, making you live a lie! So, who is worse, the up-front liar or the secret liar?

During the years I have worked with others and myself, the three main reasons I have found for the cause of suffering are:

We think that we are a separate being from God.

In this belief and feeling of separateness, we identify aspects of ourselves that we cannot accept and love.

We identify aspects of others that we cannot accept and love.

What we do not accept within us will make us antagonistic towards another. What we feel disturbed by or angered by in another is what we have not yet acknowledged and accepted within ourselves. We each have the seeds of everything within us. In some people a seed has sprouted which they have never allowed in themselves.

For example, one of my clients could not stand the way a friend of hers constantly preached his dogma. As far as I am aware, she never preached to anyone, and the idea of this being an aspect of herself horrified her. It so disturbed her that she never allowed this seed to manifest externally. If she had not judged this seed within her as something bad, she would not feel uncomfortable to see this seed sprouted elsewhere outside of her. She may then have even found her friend's preaching funny.

The fact that we judge anything, in the first place, is because we feel split from God. Therefore, we think that God will judge us, and so we judge everyone and ourselves the way we think God will.

Here, our suffering is based on ideas, concepts, changing norms, projections, and, of course, untruths. That which changes constantly is not truly real. That which is not real is not Truth. Has there been any *attitude* held by everyone in the world, throughout history, that has remained permanent? No. This proves that an attitude changes and is, therefore, only relatively real. If an attitude is not permanently real, why allow it to make you suffer? What attitude have you long held, which now feels alien, but which made you suffer previously because of your identification with it?

For example, another client has suffered a great deal because his sister married outside of the family religion. He totally rejected her, as did all other members of the family. But he misses her, worries about her, and fears that she may be punished in the afterlife. One day, he may wake up feeling differently with a change of *heart* and wonder what he has done.

Even more extreme, in India, for instance, love marriages and interdenominational as well as interracial marriages can be frowned upon by certain societies. Sometimes even members of their families murder the couples.

Happenings such as these have to do with transitory and fickle attitudes. Yet we allow these perspectives to cause us so much distress. Countries regularly go to war because of inflexible attitudes and rigid beliefs.

There are times when we are ready to face ourselves more, and to know about what needs to be healed within us. Life is an expression of God; therefore, it will bring to you the situations and people who can show you your wounds and your strengths. It will bring to you perfect scenarios, personally designed for you, in order for you to **Heal.** Welcome these opportunities.

You will meet with people who will disturb you. You will meet with experiences which will "charge" you. Whenever you feel a strong "charge" about anyone or anything, know that it is something within your own *shadow* that is being mirrored back to you. Know that this is the most perfect time for you and it is the right instance for this to happen.

Carl Jung explained the *concept of The Shadow* as all the aspects of ourselves that we had not made conscious, which we had rejected, and which we had yet to own. ***The shadow holds within the psyche all that is repressed, unacceptable, unknown and denied—that which we dis-identify with.*** It is the stuff of our projections, and in looking at their reflections in our external world we have an ideal mirror for seeing and making conscious this hidden material.

Perhaps your mother or father or early teachers instilled in you that what you desired to be or express about yourself was unacceptable but the longing remains in the shadow waiting to be satisfied. Take the case of the woman who could not stand her friend's preaching. When we talked about this, she discovered that she thought she could be a good preacher, better than her friend, and she said she felt that she could inspire people. Sadly, she realised that she had never had the opportunity to do so, except for a period in her life when she was teaching. She recognised that teaching and preaching were similar.

Welcome your shadowy part, and ask your Divine Heart to allow you to love it, more and more.

When You Discover

powerful and painful thoughts arising within you,
and you feel overwhelmed by reactions,
make a contained and appointed time with yourself of,
say, 30 minutes.
You are worth that, are you not?

Choose a time when you will not be disturbed.
Take the telephone off the hook!
Sit comfortably.
Light a candle.
This can symbolically hold the "light" for you.

With your mind, connect to your heart
and place your entire self lovingly in your heart.
Know that your heart is Divine and Vast in its Compassion.
Ask the strong feelings you are experiencing and which are upsetting you
to come closer and closer to your heart.
Feel the love in your heart towards them.
Let them be lovingly embraced by the light and tenderness of your heart's warmth.
Breathe them into your heart and then breathe them out
as transformed particles of rainbow light.
Continue daily
until you feel peace in your being and happiness in your heart.

HEAL

Your capacity to love anything or anyone is related to how much you love yourself. No one wants to start with their own self. It is easier to *pretend* to love others. It is easy to forget about oneself—much easier! It is easy to immerse yourself in everyone else's life—instead of looking towards your own. It is easy to deny that you exist and have powerful thoughts and feelings. It is easy to pretend to others that you are *feeling fine*. It is easy to deny that you need to acknowledge yourself at all. It is easy to immerse yourself in some activity, even service or volunteer work in an excuse to avoid what is really going on. It is easy to say or write:

With lots of love, much love, I love you.

But do you really know what you are saying? Do you really mean it at all? How dependent is this love on how these people continue to fulfil your expectations? How long and how deep and true is this love, really?

There can only be a true action of love for another
when there is true and abiding love for the self.

This is not the love that is self-infatuated and based on how you look, on what you have and hold, but rather it is the love and respect for That in you which is absolutely Sacred and Divine. There can only be respect for another in this way, when there is total respect and honesty for oneself.

For One Moment

just pretend
that you have fallen in love with yourself.
There is no one in the world like you.
There is no one in the world that you could possibly
love more than you.
You are a precious, beautiful, Divine gift of God.
You are wonderful, and oh so beautiful.
You are everything and everyone that you could ever need.
You are Divinity Itself.
For just one moment,
hold yourself tenderly and feel how warm your heart is.
Cuddle in closer
and feel the beauty of you holding you.
Know that you are a delight.
Snuggle into the comforting and exclusive warmth that is you
and rest, rest, rest.
Do this every day
until you accept yourself gladly and joyously.
Do this every day
until you feel deliriously happy about you.
Do this every day
until you know that you are your best friend.

HEAL

The more that you love and respect yourself, you, who is the temple, the sacred holder of Divinity, the more everything you do will be filled with love and respect. The more you honour and respect your feelings, the more you will honour and respect the feelings of others. The more you love yourself, the freer you will be in every activity you do. This is essential for true healing. This is needed for true healing of the self and others. The more you are healed, the more you are a natural aid for the healing of others.

Love is the Healing and the Healer.

The more you love yourself, the more you can ignite that self-love in others and witness the miracle of healing in the reflection of love on their faces.

I once had the habit of smoking. I could not give it up. I had every excuse for holding on to that white and pure looking, yet dangerous and foul-smelling attachment. I had many very plausible excuses to help me retain the habit. *I am too sensitive and I need a cigarette to keep me grounded,* was one very exotic and rather glamorous one I liked to say. *It helps me breathe,* was another one I would say! Yes, at that time, I actually was aware of breathing when I inhaled. I was not really aware of breathing at any other time. That was how much I had so abandoned myself.

When I first visited India, I stayed for some months in the foothills of the Himalayas with a very kind and compassionate Tibetan Rinpoche, (reincarnated precious being) and his family. This time profoundly changed my life. But even there, in such spiritually idyllic surroundings, I could not stop smoking. I did not smoke in my room, but I did in the compound of the house.

When I went out with Rinpoche, and we had a meal in a hotel or restaurant, I would tentatively light a cigarette, holding my breath to see if there was any reaction. The very compassionate and kind Rinpoche would just smile and tell me to go ahead if I wanted to. One day, not long after I was staying in his home, I felt very bad about smoking in front of Rinpoche. It was not that he had said anything to me, or had disapproved in any way. However, I saw him as such a spiritually pure and precious being that I did not want to continue polluting him in any way with my cigarette smoke. And so, I did not feel comfortable smoking in his presence.

But this realisation also disturbed me, and I was not quite sure why. A few hours later, when I wanted yet another cigarette, the bombshell hit me. An internal voice said to me, "Where is this love and honouring of yourself?" In that instant, I knew that Rinpoche and I were one. I knew within that whatever I saw in him was also in me. *I was also precious.* So where was my self-respect and self-honouring?

Finally, I connected with enough self-love and compassion to see and feel my own abandonment of self. What a joy! I told Rinpoche that I would like to stop smoking, but that I had attempted to on several occasions, and it had been very difficult. Again he smiled and said, "I will help you." He told me that from the next morning I was to say to myself,

I am not a smoker.

It was that simple.

I have not felt the need for another cigarette since, and I enjoy so much the experience of breathing! Rinpoche showed me the power of true healing. His compassion and my loving respect for him connected me with the wonderful, whole love within me. He did not show any disapproval of me or judge me. If he had, I probably would have rebelled, or have been so upset that I would have smoked even more. The whole happening was so perfect, as everything in this radiant world is. It was the time for me to stop smoking and to truly learn from the experience. I have no judgement of myself for having smoked, nor do I regret that I ever smoked. Smoking has been a part of my learning and the experience enables me to tell this story. What joy I feel, in catching a glimpse of the wisdom and love of God!

HEAL

Respect and Serve Others and Find Love in Your Heart

In being able to respect Rinpoche I found a way of finding respect and love for myself. In respecting his preciousness and purity, I found my own preciousness and purity, and was healed of a very powerful and damaging addiction. My Guru, Sri Sathya Sai Baba says:

The proponents of Self-esteem often quote the slogan if you cannot love yourself; you cannot love anyone else. One main problem with this is that it tends to put the cart before the horse, for the converse is even truer.

As Swami points out here, one can develop oneself and one's capacity to love through the loving and the respecting of others. I personally found this out when I was able to change my behaviour because of the love and respect I had for Rinpoche

This is a very profound truth and easy to carry out. There has to be someone in the world that you respect and love. Do to yourself, as you would do unto them. Remembering this greatly helps us not to become too self-oriented, self-grasping and selfish in our searching for self-love. True self-love is not merely about caring for you. Having true self-love is having true love for others.

Self-absorption, of the selfish (non-spiritual) kind, is a huge pitfall many of us tumble into and one that is very dangerous. We can get lost in this self-world and find it difficult to find our way again. I have met many people who have been involved in a search for the self through so-called, all-consuming *growth work* such as psychotherapy, psychic development and meditation, but these do not necessarily make people more compassionate, caring or spiritual. Sometimes, in fact, they do the opposite and make us even more egoistic, self-absorbed and selfish.

Even if you want to do *service* and help others, you have to be really honest with yourself. It sounds so spiritual—like Mother Teresa. Your idea might be noble, but can you really call it *service* if you ambitiously ride roughshod and trample over others to do what you think is for a good cause? I have been on the receiving end of these kinds of ***counterfeit do-gooders***, and I have felt trampled on—both as a receiver and as somebody who got in the way of them saving others. It was pretty horrible. Maybe somewhere in my past unconsciousness I did the same to others. But I certainly hope I didn't. I hope that I am become increasingly more loving, caring and sensitive.

Our total insensitivity, our inability to see the whole picture is part of our collective sickness. For example, one man got himself into huge debt trying to satisfy his family's unending desires. He wanted people in the community to think well of him. He kept on borrowing money from his friends to feed, clothe, shelter and satisfy his family. He expected his friends to help him because he thought that what he was doing was good. In his particular community, how you treat your family makes your reputation. Having a good name brings respect. However, his total insensitivity to his friends' financial positions, and his inability to see the whole picture ended up making him sick.

He became suicidal when he was unable to keep meeting his family's needs, and realised that he could never pay back his friends. His friends felt used and cheated. Eventually, he even lost his friends. His family, once they realised he was not Santa Claus, began to abuse him. So, you see, sometimes the service you think is best is the worst thing you can do.

In India, many foreigners, with proportionately more money than the average Indian, feel compelled, out of sympathy, to give substantially much more money for services and goods than what the local people can afford to pay. They do this with the best of intentions, but it causes jealousy, hatred and corruption, not to mention higher prices where foreigners are.

Sai Baba, has also pointed out that when we give money to beggars, for example, we actually take on their karma. If they buy alcohol or harm themselves it is not only their fault, but also our ignorance which caused this to happen. The compassionate thing to do, Sai Baba advises, is to give food, clothing and shelter.

This acting in ignorance is our pain, and it is a result of our separation from the truth of us. Our compassion cannot be so misdirected, as in the above examples, if we have true respect for others and for ourselves. We have to be vigilant in looking out for our genuine motives in any of our undertakings.

A few *stop and think* questions to ask yourself before you get involved in any caring and service-oriented ventures are:

Why do I really want to do this?
Am I using or hurting another in carrying out my wishes?
How desperate am I to help?
Is there really a need?
Who else could do this better than me?
Can I afford to do this?
How is this pleasing my temporary ego?
How is it affecting my immortal soul?
Is this pity or compassion?

Perhaps all of your efforts are merely to satisfy your own needs in a big way, and have nothing much to do with selflessness. If you are affecting anyone else in a way that is causing upset, then you are hardly doing *service.* It is more likely your need or ambition in your own chosen way, and you are really only serving yourself.

These questions are important for us to ask ourselves when we are on the spiritual path. Many who enter into seeming spirituality merely become zealous, ambitious and grasping. They have a vested interest, and they are on a mission. They want to be recognised and honoured. In actuality, these are all the things spirituality is asking us to let go of. When we do *service* selfishly, one day our world will fall into pieces around us. And it will be too late to ask, *Why*? We will have to ask, *How do I begin to rectify?*

The point is that we bring all our neurotic issues with us wherever we go, even on our spiritual paths. And sometimes the *energy* we gain through thinking that we are doing so well in our so-called *service* actually intensifies our neuroses and ego-power. We have to want to love ourselves enough, we have to want to love others enough to keep pausing and finding out how honest we are.

It is these underlying and motivating conditions within ourselves which are the root of our pain and disease, and they are sometimes perpetuated, made even worse, in the various, and sometimes limited healing methods we seek out. We then ask, *Why don't I HEAL*?

In many kinds of New Age therapies I have yet to see the idea of loving others compassionately or in a caring way emphasised or even included. Is this really healthy? In fact, New Age therapists teach some people that they should never undertake to do any kind of service-oriented work, such as making bandages for lepers, without charging a fee! *What's in it for me?* They are told to ask themselves before doing anything. If there is nothing in it for them, they are advised not to do it. They are told that this may make them feel resentful. This way of becoming more individualistic, but less spiritual is the new religion.

Even if we cannot feel love for another, we can at least try to be respectful, courteous, kind and, if appropriate, even helpful. We also do not need to be friends with everyone. There are, in fact, some people we should never befriend. But we can refrain from hurting anyone. The more we realise that others feel just as we do, go through the same experiences, have the same hurts and happiness, the more we can be increasingly open to others in a loving and understanding way. In this way we will develop respect for others, treating them, as we ourselves would like to be treated. To do this is a true act of self-love as well as true love for others.

Anger

3

"Are you saved?" An orthodox preacher once demanded of me. Saved from what? I wondered. Finding me unwilling to join him in his narrow interpretation of the truth, he shouted at me angrily, "You go to hell!" Well, what is hell if not the torment of harmful emotions such as anger? Smiling, I replied, "I may get there by and by, but you, my friend, are there already!

Other people had been listening with keen interest to our conversation, which took place on a train. When I gave him that answer, they all roared with laughter.

Paramahansa Yogananda—*The Essence of Self-Realization.*

Anger is one of the most destructive emotions we can have. It is violent, invasive and exhausting, and can make us as well as others ill. The next time you feel angry, try to witness yourself and observe, for even a few seconds, what is happening in your body. The first time I managed to do this, I felt waves of fire burning through veins in my legs and arms. I was not even that angry, I thought! But that is how seriously damaging a little anger is. Imagine what a veritable rage will do? Later, I also felt the fire burning in my solar plexus and heart. There can be no love felt when anger is present. Imagine what this does to your heart and digestion? Let your heart HEAL.

Sathya Sai Baba tells us that when we feel angry we should try to lie down somewhere in a quiet room and sip cool water until the anger subsides, or sit down and look at a mirror.

He says:

Anger is debilitating in its effect. The nerves become weak; blood is rendered warmer; its composition changes. A simple burst of fury consumes the strength gained from food during three months !

Some therapies encourage people to feel anger. We have to be careful with this. We have, however, to learn how not to repress anger. Releasing anger, by feeling it in a healing way, is a different matter. A thin, white, tight-lipped mouth and face with its inherent *cold anger* is just as damaging as an explosive rage. If unchecked, both leave a permanent imprint on the face.

Remind yourself that anger is energy and all energies move and change. Even if we really try to hold onto the feeling, we cannot! Even if we really want to remain angry with someone, it is impossible to do so. Eventually the energy of the anger will dissipate and subside. Try it. The more you try to hold the anger, the more it will seem to move quickly away from you. This is because there is no contraction, no pushing away. You are actually welcoming the feeling to come close, and to stay with you. The anger feels so accepted it just dissolves! When the anger dissolves have you noticed how it sometimes feels as though it has all been for nothing? People have often asked me when they have experienced such a situation, *What was that all about*? But, what a war zone anger leaves behind it.

Sai Baba says:

Anger is harmful; it makes you do things blindly. You will have to repent much, for whatever you do in anger; when your anger cools down, you see things clearer and then it is too late to correct the wrong you have done.

In working with my own emotions, and with other people's emotions in therapy, I find that tremendous grief is usually just below the surface of anger. The angrier we feel the more grief there is. Oh dear, our poor, poor little selves. What we need here is love, love, and more love. Grief has to do with attachment. Attachment has to do with wanting something, someone to be a certain way. Attachment is about desire and control.

When something does not happen the way we want it to, when someone is not being the way we want them too be, the grief is there. If we do not immediately *catch it* as it arises, and feel the grief (And who normally wants to?), the rush of feeling will quickly turn into anger. The angrier we are the more alienated we are from others and ourselves. The angrier we are the more we feel abandoned, for we have abandoned ourselves.

The Next Time You Feel Angry

try for just a moment to catch the grief
before it is consumed by the rage.
You do not have to understand why it is there.
You have had numerous lifetimes of childhood hurts,
being let down, abandoned and so on.
It has all happened before and it is happening again.
It is enough for you to know that you are hurt.
You need to know that if you go into this rage
you will abandon yourself further.
Do not abandon yourself.
Do not go into this Hell Realm.
Feel your hurt
and just as you would
with a small child
who is sobbing his heart out,
hold yourself, soothe yourself and love yourself.
Say to yourself, "There, there.
There, there, you poor darling.
You are so hurt inside, that is why you are upset.
Never mind. I love you
and everything is going to be all right."

HEAL

As long as we feel that we own, or can own, anything or anyone, we will have attachment. As long as we expect someone or something to be a certain way, we will have attachment. As long as we seriously take this world as concrete and solid, we will have attachment. As long as we think that our personality and body will live forever, we will be attached. These attachments will one day hurt us and potentially make us angry.

When we realise the truth of this world and its impermanence and transience, we cannot be angry for long. We then realise that our anger is based on illusion. Buddha said in His first teaching that the root of all our suffering in Samsara *(the cycle of birth, death and rebirth)* is ignorance. Ignorance, until we free ourselves from it, can seem endless. Life is as brief as a lightening flash, a whisper of time, so why do we take it to be so permanent? Why waste the precious gift of this time in wanting something or someone that can never be yours anyway? Whatever we have will one day leave us or we will be the one to go. Is anything then worth fighting over? Is there any point in trying to hold on to anything in this material world? Why not hold on to THAT which can never die which has never left you, and which will be with you always? The rest is just a play.

The Angry Renunciate

There is an old Indian story of a Sadhu (Renunciate) who gave up everything in his worldly life to find Self-Realisation. He travelled far into the hills of the Himalayas seeking solitude and peace. He found a spot and stayed there. Years passed. Each day, he sat on a large boulder by the holy Ganges, watching the sacred river flow past him. Now, one day, he was called to the town for a short time and when he arrived back as usual to his boulder he found, lo and behold, another holy traveller already sitting there. The Sadhu felt angry immediately. How could someone else sit there? It was his boulder. He sat there everyday—he had been sitting there everyday for years.

There resulted a violent argument between the two holy men and neither would budge in their stance. God appeared before them and told them how foolish they were. They had left their families, wealth, friends, towns, everything to quarrel over a boulder. They had left everything behind, but not their attachment! All their Sadhana (spiritual practice) had come to nothing.

One Simple Practice

I do almost daily
and especially on the days when the going gets a little tough,
is to consider my moment of death.
I see myself just as I am about to leave my body.
I ask myself,
"What was that all about?
What am I taking with me?
Do I have peace?"
Usually this helps me to get things into perspective.
Try it.

HEAL

Sai Baba says:

Do not use poisonous words against anyone, for words wound more fatally than even arrows.

To **HEAL** we need discipline; we need boundaries, containment, practice and vigilance. The next step, if you have not yet taken it, is to try to be as aware as possible of what you are doing, saying and thinking at all times. Watch yourself—with compassion, please.

You hopefully read the Chapter on Self-Love first and it was no accident I put that chapter before this one, because at times the going will be a little choppy. You may discover some things that you do not like about yourself, and which you do not wish to accept. It is then that you need to remember to be kind with yourself. Sometimes you will forget that you even made a commitment to observe your actions, to being more disciplined! One minute you will be aware of going to do this, and the next you will have completely forgotten.

When you *wake up* again and realise your mistake, you can be kind and playful with yourself.

Oh Dear !
Look how I went to sleep and I forgot.
Look how easy it is to become unconscious.
Never mind.
Let's try again.

It is important to have that loving feeling about yourself and your mistakes, or you will not be able to go very far without becoming more wounded, by your own poison arrows.

Many people I work with do not get very angry with others, but they really get very frustrated and angry with themselves. They are so hard on themselves that it hurts me to watch them. I have seen people fall and hurt themselves, and then slap themselves in rebuke. I have watched people do the same thing with relationships and work situations, then mentally slap or abuse themselves. I have heard people say to themselves about themselves, *I am stupid* or *I am so ugly* or *you silly bitch.*

Who needs any enemies with a constant companion like this? Sometimes, as I have listened to these people whip themselves, I can feel the tears well up in my eyes, and I experience pain in my heart at their coldness, hardness, ruthlessness, or rage at themselves. It is very sad.

This must be, I feel, the most excruciating pain for God. If I can feel such heart-felt pain, I wonder how God feels it? I want to soothe these people and say, *Oh please don't do that. Please don't say that.* Sometimes when it has been appropriate I have.

In therapy sessions, I have, as a therapist, been able to mirror some of this pain back to people in a session, and this has helped them to see some of the their self-violence. I allow myself to visibly tremble or show my shock. Sometimes, tears have fallen down my cheeks. Sometimes people are so startled when they see me mirror this back to them, for they have no awareness of what might be upsetting me. They have become so cut off and blocked from how they are even treating themselves that they do not even see it when I react. But, when they do realise, this helps them to immediately begin to **HEAL.**

This self-anger is as damaging as any anger towards another. We cannot possibly honour our own Divinity, our inner God, if we allow ourselves to do this. We cannot see ourselves with the self-respect and self-confidence that our Divinity deserves. If we cannot allow ourselves to make so-called mistakes, to be unique, to be human, to be in a process of learning, we cannot live. We need to be able to forgive ourselves to allow ourselves to grow in life. How do we grow and mature? We usually do so by experiencing how it is *not* done! Through these experiences we learn how to develop discrimination and a confidence in our Conscience. As our Conscience is able to speak to us more clearly, we are on our way! But, like a loving mother we need to teach ourselves to be firm and how to learn self-control.

Discipline needs to be loving and caring. When a child makes a mistake, *the loving mother* does not rage or shout or hit her child, but explains soothingly and calmly and with *respect* how one should be and how one should not be. When the child is hurt, she does not further hurt it by scolding or beating. She says tender words and explains what went wrong. She is firm. She loves, regardless.

Discrimination and Vigilance

Anger produces delusion.
Delusion confuses the memory and understanding of things;
from this confusion of understanding follows
the disintegration of the power of discrimination;
with discrimination gone, the man perishes.

***Bhagavad Gita*–II-63**

I stayed for more than a year in Lucknow and daily attended Satsang (the good company of spiritually like-minded people) with a Self-Realised Master called Poonjaji, affectionately known by his devotees as Papaji. He was an enlightened disciple of Bhagawan Sri Ramana Maharishi (a great Indian Saint who taught Advaita—Nondualism). Poonjaji left his body in 1997. He frequently mentioned two words in his teachings; *discrimination* and *vigilance*. They are both essential in any self-realisation, in any true healing. He told me that discrimination was all I needed to be Free! It is all any of us need to be Free.

Poonjaji made me listen deeply to the word *discrimination* with his statement and its meaning. Since then it has been with me as one of my travelling companions. It is teaching me how to look at things, and how to determine what is real and what is not, what is worth having and what is not. In order to do this, I need vigilance. This word is also a companion. It has taught me that I should not waste a moment. We do not know how long we have to live. We have only now. I say to myself, *Do you want to leave your body feeling like this?* My response is always, *No. I want to be Freer.* This gives me the sound motivation to stay awake at the *Samsaric Wheel*—The karmic cycle of existence marked by birth, sickness, old age, death and rebirth.

This Is What You Need to Do:

Be a witness and watch you.
Try not to be too involved with what you see.
Be as non-judgemental as possible.
Observe as though you are watching a play.
Ask to feel compassion for everything you see.
Listen to what you say.
Look at what you do.

As you watch confirm to yourself that you are a Divine Being.

HEAL

Also, Especially to Help Break a Bad Habit!

Watch how you react to you.
Try to "catch" the feeling of when you are frustrated or angry or hopeless about you.

Try to catch when you are careless with your body or your health.
Catch when you punish yourself or push yourself too far.
Catch when you hate or despise you.
Catch the feeling when you are so removed from you that
you do not exist.

Attempt not to be angry,
frustrated or self-denying with anything you find.
Only stop, hold and soothe, saying soft words.
Visualise what you feel the Divine Mother looks like,
or any Divine Loving Being you feel connected to.
Visualise being held by Her/Him in loving arms.
Let Her tell you that you are doing fine,
that everything is going to be all right.

For this is true.
Everything is all right and always will be.
Everything is perfect and so are you.

Anger cannot live in softness,
only in a hard shell.
Come out, come out, wherever you are,
find those tender arms,
extending, reaching towards your troubled, fearful heart
waiting for you,
forgiving you,
soothing you.
They waited so patiently for you.
Now you can let go.
Now you can rest.

HEAL

Fear

4

Here is an old Indian story I have heard Sai Baba tell:

A Sanyasi (Renunciate) once met the Cholera Goddess on the road, returning from a village where she had thinned the population. He asked her how many she had taken into her lap; she replied, "Only 10. But, really speaking, the casualties were a 100." She explained, "I killed only 10, the rest died out of fear!

Paramahansa Yogananda told of a story of:

A woman student who used to visit Swami Shankara. She would come to him with fears and doubts. "What if this should happen?" she would moan, or, "What if I should do that?" One day this woman said to him, "But—supposing I die?" Shankara looked at her calmly and said, "All right, then, die!"

And the woman fell lifeless to the ground. Paramahansa said, "It wasn't that Swami Shankara was responsible for her death. He simply allowed her own thought-force to materialise at last, as it would have done much sooner without his blessings. Thus, her soul received a severe lesson, which the Guru had been trying in vain to help her to learn by gentler means.

Paramahansa Yogananda—*The Essence of Self-Realization*

Spiritual teachings reveal to us the fact of impermanence. It is an absolute certainty that you will die, but you do not know when you will die. This is the truth and we have to live with this uncertainty. But, like the two stories above illustrate, why let yourself be killed because of fear?

It is absolutely certain that nothing in this material realm will stay the same. It is an absolute certainty that you will not stay the same, nor will your attitudes, feelings, ideas and passions. Not even your fear can stay the same! Given the truth of this, why fear? Why allow yourself to be bound and harnessed by what is, in reality, such an illusion?

We really do not know what will happen to us at any time. Perhaps it might be something awful and terrible. Perhaps it may turn out to be something beautiful. But all that has not yet been realised is a conjecture of the mind. Do you really want to live whatever life you have with such a crippling, internal handicap?

Rosie's Healing

I worked for more than three years with a patient named Rosie in Edinburgh. She had a disease, which was rare and progressive. It affected her ability to walk and to do certain simple tasks. During the time she came to me for weekly healing, it was as though the condition was arrested, and there was a slight physical improvement. As Rosie wanted to come for healing weekly, because this made her feel better, we continued. I eventually left, however, to live in India.

On one of the occasions when I returned for a visit she came to see me. I was staying in Edinburgh for a few weeks. She asked me if she could see me while I was there, as she felt that she really needed some help. For the first time since we had worked together, Rosie was able to talk of how much fear she had within her about her illness, and how it affected her in many ways.

She gave me an example of one of the ways she was frightened. She said, that when she went out for a coffee in a restaurant and someone sat next to her, who in any way looked handicapped or disabled, she could not bear it. She talked of the repulsion and the fear she could feel just by their presence. She told me of how this fear clouded her entire life.

With the kind of condition Rosie had, there was no knowing how long she had to live. She knew that she could live to become a very old lady, or die suddenly at any time. She spoke of her terror of dying, and of how other people who were also handicapped would mirror her own imperfection and fragility back to her. These reflections horrified her so much that she did not want to go out at all in case she met someone like herself. Not surprisingly, because she was so pre-occupied with this thought, everywhere she did manage to go, Rosie would meet a handicapped person!

In Sikkim, when I was staying with Rinpoche, I was introduced to some powerful Tibetan Buddhist healing meditational practices. One of these was called the ***Tonglen Practice—the Practice of Giving and Receiving.*** *This practice is a way of bringing close to you, of welcoming even, that which you fear or want to push away. It helps you to face your fears, so that you can be healed. It powerfully helps to purify the heart and awaken compassion. When we do this, no fear can exist in us. Sogyal Rinpoche very comprehensively explains this practice in* ***The Tibetan Book of Living and Dying.***

In ***The Tibetan Book of Living and Dying,*** *it is revealed how the Tonglen Practice was re-discovered and taught widely. During the eleventh century, one of the great Masters of Tonglen, Geshe Chekhawa, read a few lines in an opened book in his teacher's room:*

Give all profit and gain to others.
Take all loss and defeat on yourself.

The compassion of these words so affected him that he set out to find the Master who had written them. In his search, Geshe Chekhawa, found out that the Master had died, but he was privileged to meet with one of the Master's foremost disciples who told him that whether he liked it or not, he would have to practice this teaching if he was ever to attain Buddhahood.

He stayed with this disciple for 12 years and fully studied the Tonglen Practice. During this time, Geshe Chekhawa was severely tested with many hardships, criticisms and abuse. Nevertheless, he continued his practice and this helped him through these difficulties. Because of his practice, he was transformed into a Master of Compassion, and then he himself began teaching The Tonglen Practice to others.

Geshe Chekhawa began to teach the Practice to a group of lepers. At that time leprosy in Tibet was untreatable. But many of them who did the Tonglen Practice were cured. As the news spread, more and more lepers came to learn the meditation. Geshe Chekhawa realised, as he taught more and more, that one did not necessarily need to have full faith in the Practice for it to work. Even though he taught the meditation, he himself never ceased to practice it.

It is said in ***The Tibetan Book of living and Dying*** *about Geshe Chekhawa:*

Towards the end of his life, Geshe Chekhawa told his students that for a long time he had been praying fervently to be reborn in the hell realms, so as to be of help to all the beings suffering there. Unfortunately, he added, he had recently had several clear dreams that indicated he was to be reborn in one of the realms of the Buddhas. He was bitterly disappointed and begged his students, with tears in his eyes, to pray to the Buddhas that this would not happen, and that his passionate wish to help the beings in hell would be fulfilled.

Rosie and I spoke about the meditation practice at length and although she was quite fearful about it, she decided to try it. We agreed to meet each week, sometimes twice a week to practice it and for our regular healing session. During our meetings I guided her through the meditation and then gave her healing. She also did the meditation at home every morning and evening. To begin with, she was aware of tremendous fear arising day by day. It was a testing time for her, but she had tremendous courage and she stayed with the process and faced it daily in the meditations.

About a couple of weeks before I was due to leave, Rosie came to the session and said to me, "You know, I have lost all fear." She said that it felt strange, but nothing frightened her anymore. She felt light and free. She had been tested in this, and again she felt no fear. She had passed the test! She had gone shopping and went to a coffee shop for a coffee. Lo and behold, there sat the external mirror—someone who was quite badly physically handicapped. Amazingly, Rosie did not feel repulsed or frightened. Not only that, but she joined the person, sat and chatted with him! There was no doubt that something incredible had happened.

After this experience Rosie's physical condition was still present, but there was indeed something very, very different about her. She appeared quite timid before, but now she exuded the kind of self-confidence that is in someone who is completely relaxed and happy with themselves and with their life. She was now **free of the fear** *that had plagued her for her entire life—most probably lifetimes and this was the chosen life to* HEAL.

Rosie explained to me that she felt that she had now lost all fear of dying. We were both very happy about what had happened. As she left, I affirmed to her that what she had accomplished was something truly profound and far-reaching. I talked about how we never know when we are going to die, but without fear we can really live and when it is time for us to leave our bodies, we can leave free of fear. Because Rosie had finally healed herself of this fear, she was on her way to becoming Whole.

As I went to the door with her I said something like this, "You know now that it is not dying that matters, but the way we feel as we die. I might die tomorrow, or you might die tomorrow. The important thing is that you know now that when you die, you will die free of the terrible fear you must have been born with. What you have gone through can never happen to you again. You are healed of what made you ill."

The next day I heard that Rosie had suddenly collapsed and died. She was in her early 40s. I was deeply affected by the news. Her death and her preparation for it had such a sense of perfect timing, I knew that she was, indeed, deeply evolved. And what courage! I felt great gratitude in being able to witness the beauty of the timing and events of her very special life and transition. She taught me so much. Rosie, like many others I have had the privilege to so-call help or be with in their times of healing and transition, have taught me so much.

Immediately after Rosie's passing, I was able to get in touch with two Tibetan Rinpoches and they promised to say special prayers to help her as she passed through the next worlds, and during a future rebirth—if necessary. I knew that the prayers of the Rinpoches would smooth her way. I felt blessed because I knew, without a doubt, that Rosie was happy. And I know it now.

Frequently I think of Rosie, and I remember the Tibetan Buddhist teaching that you can often tell how evolved a person is by the events surrounding their death and the way that they meet their death. Rosie left this plane of reality with tremendous courage and awareness. Her death taught me that God's timing is perfect. God provides us with everything we can possibly need, at the time we need it, and God chooses the right moment for us to HEAL. Rosie's story also reveals how we should never give up hope that we can progress, that it is never too late—and even on the last day of our life we can HEAL.

If you merely identify with your present body and think that there is nothing else, that this is all there is, then it is hardly surprising that you will feel fear. Think about it. Is that all there is to you? Can that be so?

The Next Time You Feel Fearful

try not to avoid what is making you afraid.
Face it instead.

Just for a moment,
stop avoiding and let yourself be still.
Have a cool drink or a cup of tea.
Try to take your time and relax.

Remember,
you do not have to do anything you do not want to do,
but neither do you need to run away from yourself or from an illusion.

Perhaps you really want to do something,
but there is a fear stopping you.
Use your discrimination.
Is there a good reason to be fearful in this situation?

Is it a healthy fear?
Or is it an unhealthy fear?

If you find yourself standing at the edge of a cliff,
and it is windy,
and you move away from the edge, it is sensible.
This is healthy fear.

But there is another kind of fear which stops you living peacefully,
which torments you
or holds you back.
Try to be honest and as clear as you can
and determine which kind of fear you have here,
healthy or unhealthy,
tangible or intangible,
vague but disrupting?

If you are on a precipice take some steps back and feel safe.
If you are on flat land, but it feels like a precipice,
take your time, and do not push yourself where you are not ready to go.

Be kind to yourself about your fears.
Take one small step at a time in facing them.

Help strengthen yourself with a sound healing practice like
the Tonglen Practice,
Get supportive and expert help if required.
Pray and offer this fear to God.
Ask God to help you leave this fear behind.

Remember,
you are not in a race.
You do not have to rush at anything.
You do not need to take a step in any direction,
unless you feel strong enough.

But,
just for today, try your best.

HEAL

We only need fear when we forget God. When we remember God, how can we fear anything? Sai Baba frequently says to His devotees,

Why fear when I am here?

As we can see in Rosie's story, fear does not go away until we face it and we believe in the power of something greater. Fear will actually chase us and follow us and, while we are its victims, we can never escape it. Fear will embody itself in people we meet and it will present itself again and again. I believe that your fear itself is *longing to be faced*, to be acknowledged and to be released to God. That is your fear's only escape from its never-ending cycle of terror, pain and destruction.

Sai Baba also says of fear:

There is one thing which is common and which creates fear in man. No one is without fear. If he does not fear anything else he fears death. When does this fear go away? When there is Abhayam (grace of God) fear leaves man. When do you get Abhayam? When there is Vairagyam (dispassion) or sacrifice. When does Vairagyam come? When there is faith in God. When do you know that all fear will vanish? As man doesn't have faith in God, he faces the ghost of fear. Wherever man goes, fear follows like a shadow. Who has fear? Only a person with defects. When a person has no defects, he has no fear. What is a defect? Lack of faith in God is a defect...

When we sacrifice our egos to God we also give God our fears. To sacrifice anything we need to trust.

Trust

5

One cannot HEAL *without trust.*
One cannot be a healer without trust.
What is a healer?
I have a definition.
It is:
One who facilitates healing.
Can you be a healer without trust?

What does it mean to HEAL*?*
I have a definition.
It is:
To become Whole.
Can you become Whole without trust?

Trust in what?
Trust in Love,
Trust in Wholeness.
Wholeness means Love.
Love means God.

Can you trust that God is within you and around you,
in everything and everyone?
Can you trust that you are God?
Can you trust that you are not God?

Can you trust that there is nothing out there,
that you are really on your own?

Perhaps you feel that you cannot trust anything or anyone at all, or maybe you feel that you can, but with reservation. Perhaps you feel that you can hardly trust yourself. But trust is needed in something, some truth, for healing to happen, for you to HEAL. To become Whole, we have to continually leap over the little bridges of separation within us, and find ways of repairing the damaged pathways. You need trust to jump over the edge and know that you will be held and carried to safety.

When you trust something, some happening, some truth, then *you* will get out the way and you will **HEAL.**

I once had the awesome opportunity of giving healing to my then Guru, Papaji, in Lucknow, India. I was with him in a small room to the back of the Satsang Hall. He had recently been involved in a car accident and had a badly hurt right arm. I sat at his feet and I heard my voice say to him, *Can I give you some healing*? Now where that came from I do not know! I loved and respected Papaji enormously, but like many Masters he could at times be terrifyingly unpredictable. Also, I was aware that he was the Healer/the Master and in being so, I would normally feel it too presumptuous to offer him healing! Knowing this and feeling potentially a bit like a scared rabbit wondering when I was going to be eaten, it was really the last thing I would have imagined saying. But I did.

Sai Baba says:

In all effort, if you trust in a Higher Power, which is ready to come to your aid, your work is made easy. This comes from true devotion and reliance upon God, the source of all power.

To my astonishment, Papaji agreed to my offer and I knelt in front of him and held his arm and his hand between my hands for some time. I was aware that my heart really wanted to do this. Something deep inside me trusted that what was happening was good, and I was able to continue with what I was doing.

In retrospect, I realise that I managed for that short time to get out of my ego. I did not think about whether I was making a fool of myself. I did not question the fact of how I (who felt I was in emotional fragments at that time in my life) had the audacity to offer healing to a man whom I felt was already *Whole.*

How could you be so egotistical? My ego would have been likely to scathingly condemn me. Or, *How could you possibly think you could be of any use here?* would be another possible inner tormentor. All, however, was hush inside me and I felt good. At one point Papaji looked around the room at the few other people present and said, *She's good.*

Papaji triumphantly left freely waving his formerly pained arm. But all the while I was supposedly healing his arm, I was aware that I was the one receiving. Increasingly, I have realised the strength of the healing that he had showed me in that incident, and in showing me something rather wonderful about healing. I had been working as a National Federation Spiritual Healer for a number of years, and I had also been initiated into Reiki I and Reiki II. But this incident marked a turning point for me. That day, outside the Satsang Hall, a Reiki Master who watched Papaji leave the hall and get into his car waving his arm, approached me and offered to initiate me as a Reiki Master. Trust had to be present for what happened.

Just Let It Happen

Find a comfortable quiet corner to sit in.
Light a candle
to "hold the light."
Have a pen and some paper
or your journal.
Connect with the feeling in your heart.
Think of its love
and know that you are at one with it.
Now, without thinking, examining or judging
let your hand write down words about trust.
Write a question at the top of the paper
such as
"What do I trust?"

or
"What or Whom can I trust in?"
or
quite simply write
"I trust in…."

Let your hand write an answer.
Perhaps it will write sentences or words on its own.
Do not try to change anything.
Just let it happen.

Later, look at what you have written.
Honour whatever you have found that you can trust.
Be grateful
and
say,
"Thank you."

Papaji's Story

Papaji tells us how he travelled all over India looking for a Guru:

So, I would find a teacher and ask them to show me God. Then all of the devotees would look at me and show me their long beards which they grew during their fifty-year stay with that particular Guru. They would say, "We have searched unsuccessfully for years! How do you expect to come in here with your shoes on and see God in a minute?"

Then they would push me out. What to do? But, if you search for something so intensely that you won't even take food until you find it, then you will get what you want. So, this story ends at the feet of Ramana Maharishi. I asked Him, "Can you show me God?"

He said, "No, God cannot be seen, He is not an object of senses which can be seen."

I was amazed at this and wondered what He would say next. Then Bhagawan said:

YOU CAN'T SEE GOD BECAUSE YOU ARE GOD!
HOW CAN YOU SEARCH FOR THAT WHICH YOU ARE?

*At that moment I had **full trust** that I am God and this trust didn't falter and still it stays.*

How can you say you have trust? You have mistrust. If you trusted your eyes would shine and your face would shine and you would smell a fragrance. You have to trust what you are. What is there to mistrust?

Sri H. W. L. Poonja (Papaji)—***The Truth Is***

Healing happens with trust. We do not have to understand why. Knowing is enough. How can we understand anything really in its most profound sense? Can you understand God? Can you understand Divinity? Can you fully understand Truth? But sometimes we get a glimpse of what this feels like. You know when something wonderful is happening—something greater than your mind and which is beautiful, inexplicable and wondrous. When you enter into a relationship with this Mystery of Divine Love, a miracle truly happens.

Patricia's Miracle of Trust

Many years ago, before the incident with Papaji, I had the opportunity of becoming a member of the National Federation of Spiritual Healers—a UK organisation of spiritual healers. At this time in my life, I was working as a medium, psychic and therapist, but I was still inexperienced as a healer. People had for some time asked me to give them healing and, although I would oblige and it seemed to help, I had not intended to join any organisation or become more involved in hands on healing work. I was not sure that I should do this, that God wished this for me. And so, one day, when the registration papers had been sent to me and I was considering what to do, I asked God aloud, as I sometimes do, whether I was to fill in the form. I asked God whether I could be any real help as a "healer" and, if so, to give me a clear indication of Divine Will.

Later that day, a young, attractive woman came to my door. She asked to see me and she told me that she had heard I could do healing and that she was sure I could help her. Her name was Patricia. Although she was young and looked healthy she walked with a limp and was in obvious discomfort.

She told me that she was a ballroom dancer and that she and her partner had won many prizes for dancing. But, a few months previously, she had experienced an accident. The cartilage in her knee became infected and then became damaged. She had been receiving medical treatment, cortisone injections, but there had been no improvement. Her doctors advised her that, although her condition might not get worse, there was little hope now of a recovery. She was devastated by this news. She could no longer dance, she had been unable to work and so had also lost her job. She had to wear flat shoes. Her whole life had changed and she had been given no hope of things improving.

She told me that she knew I could help her. I hesitated. Not only was I not convinced that I could be a good instrument of healing for her, I was anxious that if we tried and there was no result that this would upset her more. But, there was something about her confidence that I knew was more from her Divine self than her ego self and it just felt right. I decided that I had to trust the situation, her trust, and the timing of it all.

The session did not take very long. I held her leg and knee between my hands and I felt prompted from within to ask her to visualise what the inside of her knee looked like to her. She was able to do this very well and graphically described the wound.

As I held her knee and prayed, I encouraged her to stay with the mental visualisation and to imagine the wound healing.

Within a short time, we both heard a clicking noise coming from inside her knee. It was like, click...click...click...click...click...and then it stopped. I could also feel between the palms of my hands some movement with the clicks, as though something inside her knee was knitting together. There was a fluttering feeling underneath the skin. When everything went still, I removed my hands from her knee and asked her how she felt.

Patricia stood up and beamed a smile saying that the pain was gone, and to my astonishment, she walked back and forward without any sign of a limp and she said that she had no pain at all. She was convinced that she was cured. I was still hesitant. I was still not sure what had really happened, even though I could see with my own eyes that she was truly fine. I asked her to keep in touch with me and to let me know how she fared as time went on.

About a month later Patricia came back to see me. She was very distressed and severely limping again. She was the same as she was before the healing. The story she told me, however, was quite incredible. Since she left me on the day of the healing, Patricia had felt no more pain and had experienced no more limping. She was cured! But, Patricia had been given a prior appointment to return to the hospital for a check up and for more treatment. She wavered about going but then she thought that she should go and tell them what had happened to her and how she had healed.

No one at the hospital believed her, however. They advised her that she could not possibly be healed, that there was no way that this could medically happen. Their previous tests had proved this, they said. Not only this, but they told Patricia that she was probably only experiencing some kind of strange remission, and that during this time, walking and dancing normally could seriously damage her further. She did not believe them. They then advised her that they needed to give her more injections in her knee and that this might help her to not damage her knee during the remission. They insisted. Patricia said that she heard a silent "No—Don't let them do this to you." But she wavered again, and thought that perhaps the medical treatment might not harm her. She had the injection and, to her horror, her knee reacted violently. The return of her limping and pain were the result.

So, she asked me if we could do the healing again, and she was sure that it would cure her again. I wondered if we were tempting God's

Providence, but we had nothing to lose and so we had another session, just as before. Astonishingly, the identical clicking and fluttering underneath the skin happened again. The session took perhaps 30 minutes. When we finished, Patricia stood up and walked straight and sure. Miraculously, the healing had happened again and she was just fine!

Patricia was one of the testimonies for my healing membership application form for the National Federation of Healers. When she left my home that day she saw an advert for a shop assistant in a nearby pharmacy. She walked in and got the job. She threw away her flat shoes and started dancing again. She told me that she would never again deny her inner-voice. This was the voice she needed to trust. I am sure that this was the voice of her Divinity, the God within her.

I became a member of the National Federation of Spiritual Healers and I began a journey of discovery into Healing. I was in no doubt that God had answered me that I was to go ahead and sign-up! Working with Patricia, God had shown me, in a profound way, how true healing happens. The healing was neither up to Patricia or me. God wanted the healing, God put Patricia and me together and arranged the healing, and God did the healing. God did this with perfect, awesome timing, teaching us both what we needed to learn at that point in our lives. All we needed to do was to TRUST. We did not need to trust in each other, in professionals, even in diagnoses. What we needed to learn was to fully trust in God, and in this way, **HEAL.**

Gratitude

6

I remember hearing Rinpoche, with whom I had stayed in Sikkim, talk to a group of people in Scotland at a Tibetan Buddhist Centre. He was still relatively new to the West and the Western mind, having lived his life, up to that point, in Tibet and then Sikkim. He described a simple Buddhist Meditation on Compassion to help people connect more to their hearts. It involved sending out love to others. In order to help people do this he asked the audience to consider that all beings were like their own mothers. From the love one felt for one's mother, he said, the love was then expanded to include all sentient beings. Thus he led us into the meditation.

A little later, he asked people if they understood, and if there were any questions. A man sitting near the back said, "I don't love my mother!" He said that, because of this, he could not do the meditation. Rinpoche smiled. He was new to this kind of response, but he handled it very well. A debate ensued where Rinpoche was truly initiated into the Western mind and its habit of being quite negative, rather than positive, especially about childhood and parenting. Eventually, Rinpoche mentioned the word and concept of *gratitude* to the man—about finding gratefulness for his mother for having given him birth.

There was a silence. The man became extremely upset. He argued that he did not need to feel grateful to anyone, let alone his mother. He said that he had never asked to be born, and that he wished he had not been born. He blamed being born on his mother.

Another debate started, and Rinpoche said that being born as a human being was the greatest happening and that the man could not have received this gift of a precious human life without a mother. Rinpoche told the man that even if he did not receive any love from his mother after he was born, his mother had provided the womb for him: to be conceived, to form and to be born as a human being. Being born a human being, Rinpoche went on, was a great opportunity for the man to find his freedom from the Cycle of Births and Deaths—*Samsara*. The man eventually stopped arguing, but I do not know if he was ever able to understand and accept Rinpoches' words.

In the West, we do tend to look on the miserable side of things, rather than the bright side! We have high expectations of how things should be, and we have a habit of decrying and pushing away everything and everyone who is not as perfect for us as we would like them to be! We are often the same with our parents.

I discovered this is in my psychotherapy practice, and I began to wonder what good it really did, on a long-term basis, to keep going over the same hurt again and again in a person's experiences of childhood. This is one of the *pitfalls of so-called growth work.* Sometimes the opposite happens and people just become unhealthily self-absorbed with a seeming limitless expression of laments like, *She never did this for me. He never helped me. They did not love me.* This becomes a concrete habit of negative thoughts, which is difficult to soften.

I myself felt stuck, until one day it really became clear that, yes, there is a time to express the pain and the hurt. That is helpful. But if any true healing is to happen a deep forgiveness has to be nurtured. The eventual healing outcome of this is the feeling of gratitude.

There are different ways to view things. We can turn everything around and rather than look at what is not making us happy, or what is not working out as we would like, we can look deeply at the positive side of life. The aforementioned man could not love his mother. All right. He cannot force himself to love anyone, even his mother.

But we can attempt to feel gratitude towards our mothers for having at least given us the gift of life, and as Rinpoche said, the wombs necessary for us to enter this precious human experience.

Perhaps your mother gave you a dreadful childhood. Perhaps she abandoned you. Most probably she loved you in the only way she knew how to love, and did the best she could. But, even if she did not, you would not be alive today without her having carried you in her womb. That is something to be grateful for because this provided you with ongoing chances to **HEAL**!

Sometimes we may feel that we would rather not have been born. *I didn't choose to be born,* is something I have heard many times from clients in distress. The man arguing with Rinpoche said this. I have said it myself. But we are here and the experience has to be positive.

I worked for quite some time with adult survivors of childhood traumas—sexual, physical and mental. Some had experienced extreme deprivation and abuse from their mothers in childhood. Some had experienced similar treatment from their fathers, while their mothers stood by and took no action to help them. What became apparent to me, as these adult survivors spoke of their feelings for their mothers, was that they often loved these women who had abused them and been cruel to them. Paradoxically, I also discovered that many adults who had not been abused in childhood and who had experienced loving mothers sometimes hated them.

This led me to the conclusion that what we feel about our parents, our mothers in particular, and how we love has something more to do with us than with them. It has more to do with our wound, the one that we need to **HEAL** and which we have been born with again and again. Having gratitude can **HEAL** that wound.

Most of the time mothers do the best they can. It may not be the way we would have liked it. But how can any parenting be perfect except in the eyes of God? Only God knows what it is in your parents and in your childhood that you need to experience.

When you were absolutely helpless, who fed you, washed you, held you, and protected you so that you could have the chance of living your life? Whoever did that for you is someone you should be grateful to for the rest of your life.

The Tibetan Buddhist's teach, and it is also said different ways in ancient Indian Scriptures, that to get the chance of a human life is as rare a happening as a whale swimming in the ocean and on surfacing for air, finding a rubber ring to put its nose through. The whale dives deep into its depths and on coming up to the surface automatically puts its nose through the rubber ring that was thrown at some point in time onto the surface of the ocean. To get a human birth, it is that precise and that difficult! So, the Scriptures say that it is a terrible waste to merely spend this rare chance of human life exclusively on temporal and emotional pleasures and satisfactions, or grumbling, or worse—wanting to die.

A human birth is the most sacred one among the 84 lakhs (840,000) of different living beings in this creation. To attain such a sacred birth is a great fortune, indeed.

Sai Baba

A human birth means that the being coming into existence has the potential to know God and to know the God within. Once obtaining humanity, if one is also given parents or a home situation where morality, right and wrong and even some kind of religious education are instilled at a tender age, this is indeed fortunate and even rarer. To be able to reflect on such things, to even want to, is rarer still.

Ask yourself, *How many people in the world are really interested in the Divine or God or goodness or what life is really all about—until perhaps they are on their deathbeds and it is too late?*

To meet saints or holy people and receive their blessings, to find realised souls, is extremely rare, and to meet a Divine Being such as the Buddha, or Sri Sathya Sai Baba is like a billionth of a billionth of a billionth chance! To even hear of such people and to hear of some of the teachings is just as rare....

So, perhaps that puts our life and our opportunities into perspective. Yet, for the most part, we waste our allotted breath spans talking of nonsense, desiring, fretting, trying to understand things that really do not matter and trying to satisfy the senses. Perhaps we spend our thoughts on wanting the latest item, craving the next piece of food, longing to be rich beyond your needs, fantasising a new relationship and wishing to win the lottery. Or, we may spend a great deal of time wondering why God acts in the mysterious ways God does.

When we want, we are impoverished.
When we are grateful, we have abundance.

Sai Baba says about being a human being and gratitude:

...Only the man who shows such gratitude can be termed a human being. The ungrateful man is a demon. The human and the demonic are not different in external appearance. It is by his actions that one is called human, demonic or divine. All those who indulge in bad thoughts, bad speeches and wicked acts are described as demons. Equally, those who do harm to those who have helped them are regarded as demons.

It is difficult in our world not to behave like this. It was predicted in many ancient prophecies that the world now would be a time of Great Darkness. The Hindu Prophecies, in particular, refer to this time as the Kali Yuga—the age of Kali, the Goddess of Destruction. And, it is truly an evil time in humankind's spiritual evolution, for now a larger percentage of us are acting more like demons than ever before. In fact, Sai Baba has said that at this time there are no human beings that are fully good, as once was the case. Nowadays, everyone has some darkness in them, according to Him. This is why it is essential that we trust only God and HEAL.

Look around you at the evidence! See what are on the news stands, in the bookstores, on the television, in the department stores, in the churches, in the schools, and on the internet. There is no sacred place left. There is no place of honouring. There is no loyalty to vows. There is little respect. There is hardly any gratitude. People expect, demand and look for something for nothing. Virtual reality has become our reality and has superceded God. We have become so accustomed to vulgarity and pornography that we often do not even react. We have become so anaesthetised to our Divinity by the constant bombardment of violence, crude sexuality, and everything unholy in the name of money on all levels of our senses. We only need to see what people wear and how they act, how they fight with one another and how they treat Mother Earth and every form of life on it, to realise that humankind is on a one-way road to Hell. Millions are already there. It's not surprising, therefore, that God's pendulum will swing back into the opposite. This is what has been also prophesied. When we reach the darkest point of this Dark Age, everything will transform and we will enter the promised Golden Age. We can prepare for this now. We can **HEAL.**

Perhaps, if we just let our minds dwell on these truths, and spend even a few minutes each day in contemplation of them, this will surely help us to realise what is trivial and what is important. This will help us know what is temporary and unreal and what is permanent and lasting—what is demonic and what is Divine. This increasing awareness will internally strengthen our vigilance, help us to not waste our lives. If we do this, our children and grandchildren, as well as others we connect with, will also receive this awareness by *transmission* from us.

There is a Collective Consciousness and a Divine Unity within each of us. When we are positive, our *transmission* to others is similar to how a Guru teaches disciples through *transmission.* There is no need to say anything, argue or debate. There is space and silence when the *transmission* happens. This is the most you or any Guru can do.

On the other hand, when we are negative, the *transmission* to others is how we open the gateway for demonic forces to operate—even in the silence. So, you can see how important your thoughts are. Everything that you think and do affects everything and everyone. Billions reverberate to your vibrations. This is how evil has managed to take such a strong hold on us, but being vigilant, being positive, will be how goodness will happen again.

Knowing that *you do make a difference* can only bring gratitude to your heart. With gratitude, you ought to never feel hopeless. Every little thing that you can do in order to **HEAL**, will **HEAL** the Cosmos.

The Avatar also teaches that Devotion should be regarded as an expression of gratitude for all that we receive from Providence—the air that we breathe, the light and heat that we get from the sun, the water we drink and the food we consume. His words make me realise just how much I do get and have always received, without ever having asked. This realisation makes my heart want to burst with a feeling of gratitude and humility.

However, I sometimes forget to be grateful when I slip into *wanting* something, someone, or some happening to be other than it is. During these natural challenges of life, I too, try to remember the medicine of gratitude. Often, I go back to writing in my journal just before I go to bed and listing the things that happened throughout the day that I can feel gratitude for. This simple exercise usually brings me home.

In Gratitude

Just for a moment,
think about all the gifts you have been given in your life.
Seeing,
hearing,
touching,
tasting,
smelling,
being able to walk,
Conscience,
Consciousness,
Nature,
family,
friends,
health,
education...
The list is endless.

In gratitude,
create your own list.

Write it on a piece of paper or in a journal.
Return to this practice when you remember another thing to be grateful for.
Attempt to do this for a few minutes each day.
Try not to go over what you have written each day.
At the end of a week read what you have managed to list.
Read again and connect with how your heart feels.

Just for a moment,
affirm your gratitude.
Feel this gratitude.
Affirm your gratitude to the Divine.
Thank God for the opportunity to receive all that God has given to you.

HEAL

In gratitude,
just for a moment,
think about all the traumas
and the difficulties
you have been given in this life to experience.
Write these down on a piece of paper or in a journal as you remember them.
Return to this practice when you remember another trauma or difficulty.
Attempt to do this for a few minutes each day.
Try not to go over what you have managed to write.
At the end of a week, read what you have listed.
Try to experience whatever emotions or feelings are present
and express them appropriately,
say, by writing them down and/or praying
and offering them to the Divine Source,
or your personal Guru,
or your-Self, that One who is moving towards Wholeness.

HEAL

In gratitude,
during the next week, do a similar listing as before,
but these times think about the goodness that has come
from any of your difficulties and traumas.
Think about how you are now, compared to how you were then.
Think about what you have learned,
and how your life has changed.
Write the words down that come into your mind.
Try not to go over what you have managed to write.
At the end of a week, read what you have written.
Connect with the feeling in your heart.
With that feeling of gratitude
give thanks to the Divine.

HEAL

Show the parents respect with love and devotion. It is a tribute you should offer them for the great chance they gave you to come into this world, with all the wonderful opportunities it offers for Self-realisation.

Sai Baba

When I realised the true purpose of my life and how all that I have and will experience is a perfect part of my journey to Divinity, I began to feel gratitude in my heart for everything that has ever happened to me. Seen in this context, I can view the difficulties I have experienced, and face the difficulties I still might undergo on my journey.

Also, in my work with people and on my own life I can see how most of our attitudes and reactions are merely habits. It is our habit to try to push away what is difficult or testing. It is our habit to see these testing conditions as bad. It is merely our conditioning that causes us to see pain as bad. We get into the habit of regarding something as either positive or negative, black or white! We think that it is bad if something or someone does not fulfil our desires, and we think it is good if our desires are fulfilled. But how much can we trust our desires? In retrospect, I am grateful that some of my desires did not come to fruition. With a little more time and constant integrated awareness of my own Divinity. I hope to realise the same about some of the desires I still feel sad about, those that have not been fulfilled. And, one day I will also understand and accept what God always knows is best for me.

There is a Higher Power, a Truth that knows what It is doing and what is absolutely right for us. There is actually perfection in everything and everyone and in every time and situation. Everything fits beautifully and is in harmony with Divine Order—for all. But we cannot see this when we wear our tunnel vision, black-and-white spectacles of desire and attachment.

In conclusion, I am grateful that I was born. I know that without the difficulties and traumas I have experienced I would be unable to feel from my spiritual heart as much as I do. And, I want to feel this way more and more. I want to know the Truth more and more. That is my purpose. I wish that *everything* I experienced and will experience be an essential part of my journey home. I also want to go on record stating that I am very grateful to my parents because it is through them that I came into this world. It is through them that I have had and am having the chance to HEAL.

Before You Go to Sleep

just for a moment,
connect with your heart
and
feel, with as much gratitude as possible,
a thank you
for all that you have experienced
during the day.

HEAL

Compassion

7

Out of his simplicity and awareness the Bodhisattva develops selfless warmth. He doesn't even think in terms of his own psychological benefit; he doesn't think, "I would like to see him not suffering." "I" does not come into it at all. He speaks and thinks and acts spontaneously, not thinking even in terms of helping, or fulfilling any particular purpose. He does not act on "religious" or "charitable" grounds at all. He just acts according to the true, present moment, through which he develops a kind of warmth. And there is great warmth in this awareness and also great creativity.

His actions are not limited by anything, and all sorts of creative impulses just arise in him and are somehow exactly right for that particular moment. Things just happen and he simply sails through them, so there is a continual, tremendous creativity in him. That is the real act of karuna—Sanskrit word which means "noble heart" or "compassionate heart."

Chogyam Trungpa—*Meditation in Action*

I have experienced this compassionate, Divine Love on so many occasions from my teachers. The occasions are almost too numerous to mention. But being graced to be on the receiving end of this incredibly accepting, creative Divine Love has given me a taste of what is my birthright—what are all our birthrights. Our spiritual path is the inner journey and realisation of our Bodhisattva natures, our natural and true Loving Selves. Everything else we experience, short of this, is a falsity and has nothing much to do with who we ultimately are.

Bodhisattva is the Buddhist term for the one who journeys on the Path of Compassion. And a Bodhisattva is a person who either has completely realised that He/She is Compassion incarnate, or who is moving towards that realisation. But we are all on the Path of

Compassion, whether we are aware of this or not, and this is the final realisation of ourselves as Love. We are all budding Bodhisattvas.

My Guru, Sai Baba, has shown me this Love in the subtlest of actions, as well as in the more overt and obvious ways. But each time I have had no doubt that I have been the recipient of His compassion. One knows when one receives this comforting, soothing, kind of Love. It cannot be mistaken for any other kind. When I am aware of Swami's compassion I realise that why I feel so cared for is because He does not expect anything from me.

The first time I saw Sai Baba it was for a brief moment and from a distance. It did not mean much to me then. Neither did I feel any connection with Him or that I should see Him again. However, a couple of months later, my life was transformed by Him appearing to me in a very vivid dream as The Embodiment of Compassionate Love.

The Invitation of Love

In the dream Sai Baba, whom I had only briefly seen and who had not yet meant much to me, meets me outside a hall. It is dark and it is as though I was waiting for someone. He comes to me radiantly shining in the very vivid orange robe He usually wears. The street is grey and darkly lit but He glows. Sai Baba stands in front of me and takes my hands in His and holds them looking into my eyes.

I have never felt such love before. It is immense. It is so vast that I cannot describe it. But, every cell of my being feels that Love. I am aware of the tenderness in His eyes as He looks at me. The dream goes on and He invites me to see Him in Darshan (where one gets a chance to view God, face- to-face) later that evening.

"Come," He says. "There is a place for you."

When I awoke, I felt as though I had been given the most tremendous healing. Of course, I had. Also, it was the beginning of an awakening of a deep devotion in me for Sai Baba. Such is the power of Compassion that it pulled me to revisit Him. Not long after the dream my husband and I returned to Puttapurti. The trip is an approximate 18-hour drive from our home in Kerala. This time we stayed with Him longer. Each day we attended Darshan we were aware of this Love pouring into us and transforming our hearts.

Each time I have gone to see Sai Baba I feel the deepening of my devotion more and more and in many different ways. But, I have only been able to do this because of the Healing Light of His compassion for me. And, the gift of this compassion in turn, leads me towards an increasing desire to experience and realise this Love within my own heart.

What can the evil effects of Kali Age do to a man whose heart is filled with compassion, whose every utterance is truth and whose body is dedicated to the service of others ?

Sai Baba

There was mention in the last chapter of the Kali Yuga and its destructive effects. As Sai Baba points out, one sure way of protecting oneself from the evil of this age is the cultivation of compassion. This age has a powerful momentum to take us into darkness and hate. When we have compassion it is difficult to feel anger or hatred at any one or anything for very long. Our basic nature is one of Love. This is recognised in almost every spiritual philosophy and culture. Compassionate Love is what every being longs to feel and to express.

Recall times in your life when people have given you this kind of affection and understanding and how it made your day so much happier, your hospital stay better, or even your shopping a more joyous experience.

Schooling in Compassion

As a child I had difficulties at school. I was very sensitive and could detect an untruth, falsity, or a deception very easily. This made me withdraw or react to people in a way that could be very alienating and uncomfortable for all concerned. I did not know how to pretend and make things better for myself. In retrospect, I realise that although I was sensitive, this sensitivity was more about my reactions than about others' reactions. But, I was not yet compassionate enough to consider how they were feeling about my reactions to them. This often made a spiralling, hostile or difficult situation. The result was that my teachers did not understand me, and, in fact, quite disliked me. But in their antipathy, I could not understand what they were teaching. I dreaded going to school and every day was an ordeal for me. I literally panicked each time I entered the classroom.

When I was asked a question by any of them, I would rarely be able to answer, and I would be either ridiculed or punished. On one occasion, I even fainted when the teacher asked me some simple mental arithmetic. I was so terrified I could not think. My mind would not function and I could not find the answer. Everything became a blur and fuzzy and I passed out.

As time went on, the situation got worse, until I was eventually put at the back of the classroom, as much out of the way as possible. I was an outcast. Children are quick to take up such messages from their teachers and so the other children in my class and school also gave me a hard time or ignored me.

The 11 plus qualifying examinations were to be held and, of course, my teachers felt I had no chance at all of passing. These were national examinations to test the I.Q. of a child at the age of 11, and they also determined which secondary school one would attend. The school a child went to at the age of 12, of course, determined what chances the child would have in further education.

I remember sitting at the back of the class watching my teacher try to show the children what kind of questions they might get in this coming examination and how to answer. I was not included. The children at the front of the class seemed to have some difficulties, but I listened in and thought that this was the easiest thing I had ever heard.

On the day of the examinations I was finished before everyone else, and I felt that it had been effortless and I had even enjoyed it. For the first time in my young life I had enjoyed a series of examinations. When the results came, I had come first, not only in my school but I was one of the first girls in the city. Everyone in the school was shocked at my apparent high I .Q. and placement. Strangely, my parents were not shocked. They knew I was bright, but they had never understood how I had not managed to shine with schoolwork.

A short while later my mother spoke with my teacher. The teacher expressed her great astonishment at my success and my mother said to her, "Yes, but it was not with any help from you." The teacher replied, " I have never been able to get along with her. She would just look at me through her spectacles as though she could see right through me and I never felt comfortable with her."

Unfortunately, as was the custom in those days, this teacher had been my main class teacher for nearly all my primary education. Because of her fear and lack of compassion towards me, and because of my suspicion and lack of compassion towards her, we created a situation that was quite devastating, I am sure, for both of us. This is the power of a closed and judgmental heart.

I was assigned to a good secondary education, but I had a lot of catching up to do. One of my first teachers in the new school was a teacher of mathematics who had a very open heart towards me. I was aware that she just accepted me. This was something I had never received before at school. Although I could hardly do more than basic counting when I first joined her class at the age of 12, I soon became first in my class in Algebra and Geometry. I know I was able to do this because of her love. It was obvious that she loved to teach and she loved us, her pupils. I knew and felt that she loved me. I flowered under her supervision, and I also was able to open my heart more in the classroom. Sadly, she left the school within a couple of years, but she helped me make the transition I needed to make. Through her love and compassion I had, for the first time in a school setting, experienced what it was to **HEAL.**

The Dalai Lama says about education and compassion:

In education, it is my experience that those lessons, which we learn from teachers who are not just good, but who show affection for the student, go deep into our minds. Lessons from other sorts of teachers may not. Although you many be compelled to study and may fear the teacher, the lessons may not sink in. Much depends on the affection from the teacher.

The Dalai Lama's Book of Wisdom

Imagine this affection and openness of heart, and even the desire to express it, present in every human being, in every setting. If this were the case, our world would indeed be heaven on Earth. Our hearts, whether open or closed, make the difference in our feeling that we are in either heaven or hell. It is that simple.

My childhood school experience of hell did, however, help me to realise that it is our hearts that matter. I realised how as a frightened and alienated child, my heart was too closed. Perhaps I was merely mirroring my teacher's closed heart. Still, I cannot blame the teacher for my years of suffering under her care. In fact I sometimes feel grateful for the experience because it has taught me so much. This is one of the realisations that has helped me to look for, find and follow a path where my heart has the opportunity to fully open and HEAL.

Compassion

does not choose when to love.
It just loves.
Compassion is like that.
It feels as though it grows and grows
for it is limitless.
There is no end to it.
There is no picking and choosing.
It is for everyone and everything.
There is no beginning to compassion,
only a rediscovering,
for our heart has always been.
Nothing can stop our compassion
from finally revealing itself,
for it is not dependent on anything.

Nothing can destroy it.
Even when we can feel so closed
that we are not aware of it,
nonetheless,
compassion is always there.

When Swami (Sai Baba) begins a discourse He addresses those present as, *Embodiments of Love.* He is telling us that we are Love. We are Divine Love. We are Compassion. Everything else that we feel which does not include compassion is a falsity in us, a lie, which pains us and is our suffering. If we can remember this, then regardless of how closed we feel at any given time, we are always near to reaching the Truth and being It.

When you think about it, it is only your giving of and receiving of conditional love—love that expects something in return that repeatedly hurts you. Conditions can arise when the one who claims to love is non-accepting, jealous, insecure, judgmental, righteous and so forth… But God accepts us fully without imposing any conditions. The awareness of this alone allows us to increasingly feel Divine Love in our own hearts. We will feel this Love in its complete fullness because it has always been there and can never leave us. It is our birthright and our Divine inheritance.

Compassion is Divine Love. But, if you find it difficult *to know* compassion in you or what it is—compared to conditional or infatuated love, try to begin by cultivating what the Buddhists call *Loving-Kindness.* This is not about having to love but to just be kind. It is about not being hurtful or inconsiderate to others, or going out of one's way to be difficult. Even if someone is not being very nice to you, do not be unhelpful. Be kind, regardless.

Being Kind

Just for a moment,
*connect to the word **kindness**,*

and send that feeling from your heart
to all the people in the world.
Begin by sending this loving kindness
to people who mean a lot to you
and with whom you feel close,
then extend that same wonderful feeling
to people who have not been so kind to you,
who have even been cruel to you.
Extend this feeling even more to include everyone,
those whom you have never met,
to those whom you are yet to meet.
Extend the feeling of loving kindness to everyone
and everything in the world,
the Earth itself and beyond,
to the countless galaxies and universes.
Extend that feeling to all.
Feel the oneness with God.

HEAL

I have been fortunate to often experience extremes. Even though joyous, tumultuous and painful, these have helped me to desire equanimity. In achieving any degree of equanimity life can be easier and happier. It is our emotional, mental and physical reactions that harm us. We react inappropriately when we do not feel equanimity When our heart is full of equanimity we have the space to feel an equal mindedness towards all. This does not mean that we love everyone. While we are identified with our egos, with our likes and dislikes and their desires and repulsion, this is an almost impossible task. But we can cultivate equal mindedness within our hearts and try not to harm anyone. If you, for example, really feel repulsed by someone, you can stay away from him/her with a feeling of compassion for both of you.

I have known people who think that they need to make the effort to love someone or like someone and so they try to do everything possible to do this. The end result can often be that in their attempts, they actually punish the person with their behaviour for they just can't keep it up! They, for example, agree to meet someone, do not really want to, but feel that they should and then spend the time feeling uncomfortable, agitated or even hostile to the person concerned. How can this be a good experience for either person?

It is true that there are situations and times when we are forced to get along with some others because of the position we are in. Perhaps we have problems with certain people we work with or who are in our family, or like my example of school. It is at these times that we can be sure that something is really being asked of us by God—something very special, which potentially will transform our entire beings.

If you find yourself in this kind of situation:

It is Helpful to Remember
that everything changes and this too will pass.
The other person has experiences and feelings as you do.
Learn how to set good boundaries and limits.
Learn what is comfortable for you.
Learn how to recognise what is not comfortable.
Try to stay within these confines.
Respect the other but also respect yourself.
Honour the other but also honour yourself.
As daily tests arise and where responses are necessary
ask yourself,
"What is the most compassionate thing
I can say/do
at this time
for him/her and me?"

Pray,
for guidance, strength, understanding and insight.
Pray
that you and he/she will

HEAL

As much as possible, during your healing towards Wholeness, you can say the following Buddhist Prayer:

Bless Me into Usefulness

I Pray that I benefit all beings
that come into contact with me.
I Pray that I will be used
to help them transform
their suffering and their lives.

Repeat this prayer when you remember it at any time throughout your day. Say the prayer especially when you feel negative and non-loving feelings toward others.

HEAL

It must be said that genuine compassion is not like pity or a feeling that others are somehow lower than you. Rather, with genuine compassion you view others as more important that yourself.

The Dalai Lama—*The Dalai Lama's Book of Wisdom*

Surrender
8

Even God surrenders to love.

Sri Sathya Sai Baba

When teaching healing methods I advise people to offer up their healing to a Higher Source of Wisdom.

Let it be Thy will and not my will.

In this way, we offer the trying, the expectation and the results of our healing to Divine Wisdom. Something very profound happens when we do this. We get out of the way. When we, our egos, do not try to do anything, we are used as vehicles of that power, which is truer, purer, wiser and greater than our egos. The healing which occurs is perfect, true and essential for the person in question. The same is true for self-healing.

Some people have said to me, *Well, I don't believe in God, so what do I do—who do I surrender to?* It's easy. You may not be able to relate to any personification of God in the here and now or in history—such as Buddha, Christ or Krishna. But, if you really think about it, there must be something or someone you are aware of which is greater than you. What about believing in pure Love, Truth, Goodness and Light? These are profound qualities which are far-reaching, powerful and transformative, and which are greater than any ego. Surely there is nothing better than to surrender to Love, to have devotion for Love.

You can offer yourself, your healing and any other action, thought, or word to this Love, Goodness, Truth or Light. The fact is that these qualities are the Truth of you. I, however, like to interchange them with the word God, which is also the Truth of you and of me.

I usually use other words too in any healing invocation I do. I find these words helpful in any prayer. In particular, I try to remember these words when I feel that I am too involved in an outcome, or when I have some kind of *personal investment* in the matter. Some additional words I like to use are:

For the good of all concerned—

Therefore, a full invocation can be,

Let it be Thy Will, not my will, for the good of all concerned.

This acceptance of God's will and God's outcome in our psyches helps us to be more compassionate, less grasping and less concerned about our egos' ideas of how things should be and how they should work out !

When we offer up our request to God for the good of all concerned, we have an opportunity to get out of the bad habits of self-seeking, self-justifying and self- congratulating. This saves us from ruin.

People I know have become exhausted and disillusioned, even ill on their *healing journey* because they think that they are the ones who have all the responsibility, and that everything is up to them! What a burden to carry !

Think about what happens when we try to stop someone from dying and they do not get any better. What happens when no amount of hands-on-healing or self-healing can cure a disease? What happens when people die or we ourselves are facing our death? Is there anything wrong in dying? Whatever gave us the idea that we have the choice of who lives and who dies or when? When you offer up the actions and rewards to a Higher Source and you surrender the idea of outcome,

you affirm that God alone knows best.

Without surrender, there can be no liberation. So long as you cling to the narrow "I", the four prison walls will close in on you. Cross out the "I" and you are free. How to kill the "I"? Place it at the feet of the Lord and say "YOU" not "I" – and you are free of the burden that is crushing you.

Sai Baba

There came a point in my life when I realised that I did not know what I was doing anymore, or where I was going. (Had I ever?) I thought I had known how to live and what to do with my life. I thought that I had an idea of what it was all about and the general purpose of it. I thought that I had been in control and that I should be in control of my life and my destiny, but no matter what I tried to do I could not get anything to work out. Internally I felt in chaos and in despair. Circumstances took me to my knees for the first time in my life. It was my first true realisation that I was helpless. I was stripped of most of my belongings. I had to live with daily uncertainty. I knew that I was fighting against all odds to have my life the way I wanted it to be. But I began to realise too that I did not really know what was best for me anyway. I realised sincerely, for the first time, that it was not going to be up to me. It never had been. I had never wanted to accept this. I wanted to be the master of my destiny.

Awakening to Surrender

I came to realise all of this in what seemed to be a matter of seconds. The thoughts felt multidimensional and as if they were coming all at once— as the Masters tell us "awakening" thoughts can be. I felt God was pressuring me into acceptance of the Divine Will. To this day, I remember the event vividly. I can still see myself as I was in that moment.

I was standing in the Library of the Edinburgh College of Parapsychology. It was a place I was to find myself in for quite a few years to come, and where I would teach classes, and learn a great deal. It was to be my training ground before I was able to take the next step.

At that point in my life I was on the brink of transforming into a new role, that of psychic development teacher, medium and healer. But I really did not want this role. All my life I had just wanted to have a family, a home, and be a housewife. Even though I knew I was psychic I did not see it positively. I thought it meant that I would have to sacrifice myself for others and I resisted it. I did not want to open my heart any more, yet it was opening in spite of me. I had longed for my life to go a different way. I remember looking upwards, as if to the sky beyond the ceiling. I realised that I had to surrender, and I said to this power which I choose to call God, All right, I give in. Do with me what you think best. I offered myself to a Higher Truth. I surrendered.

The words did not come from my mind but from deep in my spiritual heart. I did not know I was going to utter them, but I did and loudly. I surrendered fully at that moment. In retrospect, I realise that I surrendered only as fully as I could at that time. It is important to know this.

Surrender is a process for many people. It is a journey, which leads us more and more fully into the Truth. The more you the Truth, the more you are able to realise surrender. Looking back, I also realise that I had no choice. To think that you can surrender means that you think there is a choice. But, when the time is right, you have no choice. You can only surrender. You can only follow your destiny.

Years later, I had a vivid dream that showed me this truth:

The Gift of Surrender

It is Christmas time and I wish to see my Guru, Sai Baba. I know that He has a gift for me. I arrive at the Darshan Hall and there is a seat at the front for me. This means that I will be able to see Him close up. I try to sit down on the floor on the mat provided for me, but I cannot.

There is a tremendous force bearing down on my back, along my spine and from above, which is pressing my head forward to the ground. This force is bending me until I am pressed with my head down on the floor in a pose of supplication. My mind does not understand what is happening and it keeps trying to get me back up and to sit in the "correct" way, but the force is too strong. There is a struggle for some time, as I attempt to sit up and do what the mind thinks I should do. But, then I have to give in, for I cannot do anything else. I am bent and prostrate with my head on the floor in front of my Guru.

*It is only when I awake that I realise what was happening in the dream, and the gift I have received—**the call to surrender**, this force from Divinity Itself which, in spite of my mind, all the levels of my being could not deny or go against.*

Our Divinity, That within us, which is Truth, crushes us and our desires in the way worms get crushed underfoot. At this time we have no option but to die to the way we have known ourselves. To be willing and to comply with God's plan is to consciously go along with the surrender. In the end this is our only choice, and it is more comfortable than being pulled, as if by our hair.

There is the ancient story of Rama (God in form around 10,000 years ago) and His brother Lakshmana that tells of this:

The Surrender of the Bullfrog

Rama and Lakshmana, whilst taking their bath in the lake, thrust their bows into the ground. When Lakshmana later took one of the bows from the mud below, he found that it had bloodstains on it. Rama said, "Look, brother— perhaps we have hurt some creature."

Lakshmana dug into the earth and found a dying, bullfrog. Rama said sorrowfully to the bullfrog, "Why didn't you croak? We could have tried to save you. You croak lustily enough when you are in the jaws of a snake."

The frog said, "O, Lord, when I am attacked by a snake I croak, saying: O, Rama, save me! This time I found that it was Rama Himself who was killing me; so I kept still."

It is the Divinity within us, which kills our egos. Our ego-selves are like the bullfrog. When we pray, we pray to Divinity, to God, to help our ego selves and their desires. But, eventually, in perfect timing, Divinity crushes the ego itself. At this time, we can only accept and surrender. At this time we have no choice but to HEAL.

It has been my personal experience, and as a result of my knowing others' stories that when Divinity destroys, it is done with Absolute Love. The act is done in love, by love and for the sake of love. This is why, when we *surrender to Love*, we lose nothing. We can only gain more love. We cannot surrender anything that permanently belongs to us. We can only surrender what we have had on loan from God, which was never even ours. And when we surrender, God cannot resist us. God, Divinity, surrenders to us. We **HEAL**.

This is how I have experienced my journey of surrender so far. I am aware that my ego squirms and squeals and fights to stay alive. I kick, complain and grumble. But I know, that one day, like the bullfrog, I will be killed by Divinity's own hand, and I look forward to this final release from my ego-self. I can only find then what has always been ultimately mine. I can only have then what has always been there for me. When I am given the *Grace* to completely surrender, what will die is not I, but the false self, the little me concept, which has been blocking my way home.

Give all your thoughts, your worship, your sacrifice and your salutations to Me, and you shall certainly come to Me; I pledge my troth to you who are dear to Me.

The Bhagavad Gita — XVIII-65

Surrender, to me is making the conscious effort to trust God, to yield to the truth of my Soul and not to the Maya (*Illusion*) of my ego.

With Surrendering

there is no bargaining.
Only the ego bargains.
You cannot bargain with God.
God will give you what is perfect for you to receive
Your ego does not like this because your ego wants to control,
otherwise it knows it will die.
Your ego actually does not have a clue what is good for you,

only what it thinks is good for itself.
It, therefore, makes sense to follow your soul and not your ego.

The problem is
that you can fool yourself into believing
that you are following the soul
when, in fact,
you are following the ego.

Papaji once said to an enquirer who asked why she was so insecure, *Because you are depending on something that is not secure itself and, therefore, you cannot be happy!*

He gave the example of a creeper winding itself around a small plant rather than a nearby meditator who had sat for a long time in one position in the middle of a forest. The meditator thought:

This simple creeper has no trust in me, but in a plant because she knows that I am mobile and the plant is not. She is so wise to go up this small tree because the tree will not move away. She knows I will though, and when I get up she will break.

Papaji said:

No one in the world is wise like the creeper. They have faith in things that move away. They will lose their body and their life. You must learn from the creeper. Depend on something, which is everlasting, so that you are safe.

The Truth Is

I was struck, as though by lightning, on hearing Sai Baba speak in a discourse a few years ago on how we trust each day our safety and precious human lives to the keeping of bus drivers, taxi drivers, doctors and ignorant people's opinions and advise. Yet, we do not seem to trust God and place ourselves in God's hands. I was struck by the Truth of these words. We surrender to just about everything that is not appropriate to surrender to, and yet we do not easily surrender to God.

As the river surrenders to the Ocean,
surrender yourself to the Self, the Source.
And if you find that you are still swimming on
the surface of the Ocean,
stop swimming and you will sink into the Depths of Love.

Papaji

Finally

just for a moment,
contemplate on what stays True,
what can never die.
Just for a moment,
feel yourself to be the creeper
and entwine yourself around
THAT
which will not go away.
Surrender to
THAT
which will never die.

Death

9

You must live in the constant thought of God as well as of another fact, Death. The body is the car in which you are riding to Death. You may meet Death any moment, while riding; some tree or lorry or mullah or sluch will bring it. Remember Death. Remember that time is running out every moment; then you will not be tempted to waste time in idle talk or vain pursuits or wanton mischief or vulgar entertainment...

Sri Sathya Sai Baba

Implicit in death is life. Implicit in life is death. One cannot be without the other. If you spend a few moments each morning as you waken to life and think of your death, that you may die today, your life will most probably have more meaning, and you will be more present to it. On the other hand, if you let life whimsically slip by, you will find that days can go by, weeks and months even, and they will mean nothing to you. You will have drifted from the experience of one sense to another, one appeasement to another. Your life will become a kind of blur, and you will have completely forgotten its importance. *What happened and what was it all about*? You will ask as you take your last breath—*Where did it all go*?

You can spend your entire life like this. The days, weeks, months and years will haze into each other. I have met people who experience life like this. Some live to a very old age. But death always has an appointment, and the day comes when one finds oneself at the appointed meeting. If you have had a near-death experience you will understand that it is a messenger of Grace and is an awakener. Once you have had a taste of death there can be no avoiding the knowledge that this is where life and all its intricacies are leading you. Even if you have not experienced a personal dress rehearsal with death you will have experienced the death of someone close to you.

My personal knowledge of death expanded when I literally became psychic overnight. Following a series of personal shocks, my psyche was so opened up I woke up one morning able to see, hear and sense on many different levels. For example, I could peceive auras, beings in the afterlife and spiritual worlds.

A frequent experience during this time of acute awareness was of leaving my physical body. I was not always able to do this at will. However, sometimes I could. At other times when I tried to go to sleep at night, I would feel myself being unwittingly whisked out of my gross body. I would travel in my astral body, accompanied by invisible helpers and teachers, to the various planes of Consciousness—what Tibetan Buddhism calls the Bardo Realms.

These Astral or Bardo realms represent the same experiences. These are planes of relative reality where we can exist and which we can connect to on any level of our beings—even in present physical bodies. We can also find ourselves in these realities when we have so-called, out-of-body experiences and when we die.

I had no physical-bodied teachers at that time in my life, but I was aware of being taught by evolved beings from these realms that directed my many teachings. On one occasion, for example, I was taught the evolutionary process of sentient and non-sentient life forms from the amoeba to higher levels of Consciousness. My Spiritual teachers explicated this by using the Divine Force to place my consciousness into each level of being so that I actually experienced that state of awareness.

At one point I was the consciousness of a large boulder. Yet, amazingly, I could see through the millions of microscopic, porous cells of the rock. I was aware of vivid red sky above and red soil beneath me. I knew that I was not on Earth, but on a different planet. I felt an ineffable peace in this awareness of my own being and my surroundings.

However, these teachers did not allow me to enter the Absolute Divine State of Consciousness. They warned me that if I went there at that time that I would be unable to return to my then present level of reality again. In retrospect I now realise that I was obviously not ready to experience this state. It was as though there was very little time and so every moment had to be maximally used.

Later, when I was fortunate to meet my earthly spiritual teachers—from the Shamanic, Tibetan Buddhist and Advaita traditions—they validated what happened to me, what I had seen and felt. They recognised the teachings as Truth. Such instructions and experiences can happen to others under various circumstances and for various purposes.

After the first *overnight* gift of psychic awareness came to me, I began to have regular lessons. Some of these nightly psychic experiences I had were pleasant and some were not. For instance, some of the teachings were painful, harsh and shocking to me. In one Hell Realm, I experienced being stabbed by three demons. I learned how people who look innocent can actually be Evil incarnate. It was a lesson in how not to be taken in by appearances and to sharpen my survival and protective instincts.

During my nightly experiences I also met people who had died. What was revealed to me by my teachers was that the state of awareness of those who had made a transition from life to the afterlife—and their consciousness at the moment of death determined where they ended up in the next worlds. This led me to long to be more conscious of my True Self in life. For I realised that there was no avoidance, no safe place, no opportunity to go to sleep on myself, either in life, sleep or death.

Frankly, I was terrified of what I had seen and experienced during those years of nightly teachings. And so, when I first came to India, to Sikkim, I asked Rinpoche to instruct me in the Bardo Teachings from ***The Tibetan Book of the Dead.*** The following is a related story of one of the experiences I had prior to my external teachings but which made me long to search more deeply spiritually.

It was a night event, but I was not out of my body—although the person involved was !

Sleep Walking Whilst Dead

During the first few years after I opened psychically, I worked as a ***spiritualist medium.*** *I was invited to work at a large psychic centre in Glasgow one weekend, and I accepted. This work involved giving people clairvoyant reading sessions (with evidence of survival of their loved ones), as well as conducting the Sunday Service. I arrived on Saturday, and did my appointed readings. I was to sleep overnight in the same centre where the work had taken place, and where the Sunday Service would be held in the morning.*

There was a housekeeper who gave me my meal and then left for her home in the evening. I was staying in an attic flat that was part of the main building—a Georgian, with high ceilings and ornate woodwork that had seen better days.

I had a quiet evening, and I was tired from the travelling and the work I had done and so I went to bed. While I was drifting off to sleep the door of my room creaked open, and I heard footsteps. Someone walked near my bed. I could hear a man sighing. I tried to sit up but felt incredibly drowsy and almost drugged. The bed indented at my side as the unseen man lay down and turned towards me. I felt an arm come around my waist…

Because of my initial terror, my awareness speeded up and I came out of that reality. Suddenly there was no one there and I was alone. However, every time I drifted into a slower rhythm of breathing and was almost asleep, the exact same encounter happened again. Each time, I was aware of the door creaking open, the man's weary sigh, followed by the indentation of the bed and the arm about to come around my waist.

I sat up for most of the night. I realised that this man did not wish me any harm. I felt under no threat. However, I did not like the experience and so I tried everything to keep awake and to keep my energy quickened. I did this because it was obvious that he was on a very slow and unconscious level of reality. When I also "slowed down" I somehow was open to his level of reality. It's a bit like tuning a radio and finding different wave-lengths.

When the housekeeper came in the morning she asked me how I had slept that night, and I told her what had happened. She was, of course, shocked. She asked me to describe the man. Although I had only felt his presence, I had not seen him physically, but my inner clairvoyant sight had, and so I described him to her. She recognised him as her brother who had died two weeks before. A short time before he died he had visited her. He and his wife had stayed in the same room I had and they had slept in the same bed.

After hearing the housekeeper's story, I realised more fully what had happened. The man did not know he was dead. He was not really aware, at all, of what he was doing, or where he was. In his death, he was sleepwalking as though in a dream and repetitively going through the motions of one of his last memories. Now everything made sense to me.

In the service that Sunday morning, my talk was of my experience the night before and of the sleepwalking dead man. I asked the congregation to pray for him, so that he could be released from his limbo dream in order to be able to continue his journey towards the higher Spiritual Realms. We all prayed together for a short time.

Even though this was a spiritualist and psychic centre, many of the people who listened to me that morning were upset. Here, was the evidence of survival that so many of them wished for, but it was not quite in the way that they wanted to hear it. It was just too real. And I think that the most frightening thing about the story is the dead man's unconsciousness. It was obvious that he was not even aware that he had died and not only that, but he was sleepwalking, as though lost. This is not what most people want to know happens after death. They want to believe that no matter what state their minds are in when they die, or no matter how they have lived that they will find themselves in Paradise immediately, and be happy ever after.

About a week later, I was back in Edinburgh, in my home and sitting quietly in the lounge on my own by the fire. I was resting, as I had just finished a long day of work and an evening meditation and healing group in the room I was sitting in. I had only a small light in the room. Suddenly, I was aware of a bright light shining in from the hallway as the door of the lounge opened wide. I had left the bright hall light on. But as I looked at the open doorway I was amazed to see a silhouette standing in the light. I immediately knew it was the man from the psychic centre in Glasgow !

Obviously, our group prayers that Sunday morning had helped him. Now he had come to say thank you and to show me that he was free of his sleepwalking. I knew that he understood that the physical body he had been in was dead. It was gone forever. I felt his silent thank you, and then his being disappeared ***into the light.***

I was so happy to know that he was now all right. I knew a tremendous healing had happened, and I had been privileged to witness it and be a part of it. I too received healing from the experience, as it prompted me to continue my Quest for Wholeness and to more consciously **HEAL.**

There are many stories of people who have had near-death-experiences and also those that have died for short periods and have been able to return. I personally had my first near-death-experience when I was nine years old. (See *Be Happy with Prayer, Meditation and Affirmation* by Mynavati.) What they confirm is that death is not the end of consciousness, of being, and usually people who have such experiences regret the waste of their lives up to that point.

If you live with the full awareness of your impending death you will live your life with different priorities and from a different perspective. Because, as you can see, in the case of the man who was sleepwalking in death, we continue to experience in the after-death-realms where we left off in our last bodily lives.

If you die when you are drunk, for example, you may wake up in the Astral Realm with a hangover, but with no aspirin to take! And your re-birth may be to parents who are alcoholic. Nothing ends at death and this is why our lives are so important. They give us the golden opportunity to become more aware, more conscious, and more Whole. When we grasp life with this knowledge we make the commitment to **HEAL.**

Avatars, Mystics, Saints, Holy People, Gurus and Yogis, throughout the ages, have told us about the importance of life, relative to death. They cannot all be wrong. They have to be telling us something important, true and profound. Yet, for the most part, their Truth is ignored. Most people live life as though they will never die, and even refuse to think about it! Most people live as though there is no tomorrow. Meanwhile, they are not *present* today.

These Masters tell us how our God-given life is, in fact, a preparation for our death. They tell us that the purpose of life has nothing really to do with getting married, being successful in the world, having a good time, eating lots of good food, or enjoying the senses. The purpose of life is not about dying either! Animals, birds, insects can all do this.

Why is it that you have been given this rare gift of a human life?
It is to find God.
It is that simple.

These Sages also tell us that God is not *out there*, somewhere, separate from us. God is within us. So, this rare gift of human life is to find God within, and to find God in everyone and everything. All the rest of life's activities are merely dreams. When we learn to discriminate between the dreams and Reality, our false self dies while we are still alive. We become what we really are—Immortal.

What is it that you are involved in that is permanent or temporary? What is it that you will take with you when you leave your physical body and what is it that you will need to leave behind? How consciously awake or asleep are you? How much of your day are you like a sleepwalker? You need to continually ask yourself questions like these, in order to make the most of your life and prepare for your death.

The great Indian Teacher of Advaita (Non-Duality), Bhagawan Sri Ramana Maharishi, told us to live a lifetime of self-enquiry to find the answer to the question, *Who am I?* Ramana, it is said, needed to ask this question of Himself only once.

One day, when He was a boy, and on His way to school, Ramana felt that He was dying. The questions arose, "Who is dying? Who am I?" And in that moment He found the answers. He realised that He was not the body, senses, mind, or intellect. He realised that even if these died He would not. After that He went to Arunachala (a famous Shiva Mountain in Tiruvanamalai, South India) and stayed until He left his body many years later.

Buddha only needed to see one corpse, one funeral, to know that He had to leave His father's palace to search for the Truth. How many corpses do we need to see in order to know that there is a longing within us to find the Truth of our own eternal Divinity?

Without being in awe of the Truth of your life and for That which you cannot buy, hold, own, sell, taste, touch or discard, you cannot really **HEAL.** It is an impossible task. You may think that you want to heal. You may want to be a healer. But without the knowing and accepting of what your life is really for, you will potentially find yourself wasting this precious human life.

Without your belief and awareness of your own impending death and your commitment to life you cannot know what compassion is, and at best you will merely sympathise. Most likely you will become affected and upset by others and your own seeming tragedies. Viewed only through worldly eyes, your life and death will often be seen as unfair and miserable. If you have a worldly perception only, you cannot understand life from God's point of view that is Eternal.

If you are only interested in worldly happiness or reward, you will always be like a rabbit running frantically for its life from the jaws of a fox. At times you may be able to hide and pause and pant for breath, thinking that this short respite is happiness. But the chase will start again—that is, until you are outmanoeuvred or are so desperately tired that you give in to your Fate. When you find yourself cornered you have no choice and no where else to go. But, you meet your Destiny sooner and with less pain. You can ask yourself now,

Who is it that is running and who is it that doing the chasing?

and you can HEAL.

Begin the Journey

Just for a moment,
take some time to pause
and
ask yourself
the question
"Who am I?"
Begin the journey.

HEAL

Thank You for My Life and Death

When our home was in Kerala, my husband Sudevan and I had a garden, which was a haven, not only for us, but also for many kinds of birds and animals. The garden was to the back of a temple pond and the jungle was nearby. Herons would sit high on the coconut trees, and kingfishers by the well. Eagles would fly to nearby nests on tall palm trees and there were often wild cats and snakes. We kept goldfish and carp and other small fish in ponds and had many pigeons, hens, and also some dogs. We saved hens from a nearby battery hen farm in order to give them a better life and we looked after them until they hopefully had a natural death. There was an abundance of life in this garden. But, we also experienced death almost every day either with one of our own animals or birds, or wild ones.

Sometimes, we seemed to be trying to save lives throughout the day, giving our little friends treatment or placing them on our altar as we found, say, a little bird dying. We always tried to respect their deaths in this way and would have a ceremony of cremation, offering our prayers to God for their transition and possible rebirth.

At one time we had two ducks staying with us in our garden, which we had managed to save from being butchered. One was an old female who had seen better days and the other a young male who was very handsome. They loved each other very much and were inseparable. They were the only two ducks in the garden amongst a number of hens and roosters. We called them Mr. and Mrs. Duck. We did not know how old Mrs. Duck was but at times she appeared so weary that we wondered how much longer she would live.

Each evening, Sudevan made sure that all the tame birds were locked up for their safety. There was a large coupe made of wood, about the size of a small bedroom and it was adjoining the back kitchen window. As we lived on the edge of the jungle and there were prowling bobcats and wild dogs at night, as well as other predators, we always tried to be careful with the ritual of locking the coupe. The hens, roosters, pigeons, doves and ducks slept there at night.

One night after we put them all to bed, my husband opened the cage door again to count the pigeons and make sure that they were all back from their day's flying. The cage was then finally locked for the night.

The next morning we were awakened by Mrs. Duck quacking loudly, sounding in distress. She was in the garden near our bedroom window. We felt confused and wondered how she was in the garden because she should still have been locked up. We looked out the window and saw that she was on her own. There was no sign of Mr. Duck.

Later, when we went outside, we could not console her. Sudevan looked everywhere for Mr. Duck but could not find him. Eventually, after a further search, he sadly found Mr. Duck dead in a corner of the garden with his head decapitated. (Normally, this is how a bobcat kills its prey.) Somehow, the two ducks had got out of the cage through the night and this tragedy was the result.

We could not understand how this had happened, and then we remembered that after they had been put to bed for the night, my husband had opened the door again to count the pigeons. We realised that the ducks must have walked out, completely unnoticed by us. If this is how it happened, it was indeed rare for birds rarely move in the darkness. But if one walked out, the other was sure to follow as they were always together.

My husband felt terrible and he blamed himself for the calamity, for not noticing the ducks leave the cage. As was usual, Sudevan made some preparations to cremate the young duck's remains. He laid Mr. Duck on top of a pyre of some other things that were to be burned. Just as Sudevan reached for the matches to light the kerosene poured onto the pyre, a gentle breeze blew a piece of paper from the nearby rubbish bin onto Mr. Duck's body. It lay across his body like a wreath. On the piece of paper in large boldly typed letters was written ***Thank you.***

We knew without any doubt that this message was from Mr. Duck, and that it was from That in him which is Eternal and which is at one with the Divine, with God. We felt such wonder and joy to receive and experience Mr. Duck's message. Sudevan felt overwhelmed by the duck's love and gratitude and the compassion of Divinity. The miracle message took all thoughts of guilt away. **HEAL.**

I have been taught by Tibetan Buddhist Masters, and Hindu Masters as well as my Guru Sri Sathya Sai Baba, that our thoughts in the last moments before we die, are, importantly, the vehicles of our future experiences in the after life and rebirth.

Your last thought bubble is the bubble of your next birth...

This awareness alone, has made me think about death, if not constantly, with at least a sometimes awareness of its sacredness, its potential and the need to prepare for it. If we die with a feeling of hatred, we will be born into hatred. If we die with a feeling of love, we will be born into love. If we die with a longing to be with God, we will go straight to God. Life itself is the arena for this preparation. Your moment of death is potentially one of the greatest moments for you to **HEAL.**

Sai Baba says:

Life is eternally stalked by death. But man does not like to hear this. It is considered bad luck to even hear the word; even though every living thing is, every moment, proceeding nearer and nearer to that event. When you are intent upon a journey, after you purchase your ticket and board the train— whether you sit quietly, lie down, read or meditate, the train will take you to the destination. So, too, at birth each living thing has received a ticket to the event of death and is now on the journey. Whatever your struggles, safeguards or precautions, the place has to be reached some day. Whatever else may be uncertain in this world—death is certain. It is impossible to change the law.

When You Awaken to Life Each Morning

just for a moment,
imagine,
that this may be your last day in this body.
Connect with a feeling of love in your heart,
and finish any unfinished business.
Let go of regrets,
and forgive those you have not yet forgiven.
Thank everyone and everything for what you have received
and for sharing this time, this life with you.
Thank God
for loving you so much to give you this life,
this rare opportunity of preciousness.
Prepare to enter life or death.
Step into the uncertainty of the day
with God,
full of trust,
in
readiness,
happiness,
surrender,
love
and
peace.

HEAL

PART II

Some Practical Things to Do

Healing and Wholeness

10

The following chapters are various methods you can use to **HEAL.** But, healing is not just about remedying a particular emotional, physical or spiritual condition that is causing us pain or unease. Remember, earlier in the first chapters, we spoke of healing as a journey towards Wholeness. This is not to say that different ways of healing cannot help heal splits within us. There is plenty of evidence to show that they can and do. But, if we look at healing in a fragmented way, usually when one split within us is healed, another one, an even deeper one, will manifest. We need to remember that no matter how deeply intuitive, inspirational, or spiritual the method or the practitioner, this is but part of our Divine movement towards Universal, Cosmic Oneness, towards Wholeness

In accordance with perfect Divine timing you are becoming whole and complete. Even if you are not aware of it, or you doubt this truth, you are fully in this continual process of healing. This healing is taking you towards your *awareness* of your own Wholeness. We are all propelling in different ways, at different stages, and at different times towards this completion of ourselves.

I say *awareness,* for you are *That* already which is perfect and whole. As you are ready to heal more and remove the cataract of ego that blinds you to the vision of your True Self, the illusion will fall away and you will realise this truth. This lie and the mirage that you identify with, as *you* now, will one day naturally fall away as autumn leaves fall from the trees.

If there is any question as to your *healing*, your at-one-ment with your complete self, it surely is about *when* and *how* rather than *if.* The journey of your life is a reflection of your Divinity manifesting. At some point, when God wills this to be, your Divinity will manifest in its completeness. Although your journey, according to the Masters, is only a dream and is illusory and tempts you to feel separated from your Source, this is a lie. The illusion, the false self, can appear to be contaminated, but Your Divinity cannot and never will be tainted, impure or diseased. It is, has been and always will be Perfect.

In the ***Yoga Vasishta, (The Supreme Yoga)*** the sage, Vasishta, explains to Rama:

This supreme self cannot be realised, O Rama, by means other than wisdom—not indeed by exerting oneself in religious practices. This self is neither far nor near; it is not inaccessible nor is it in distant places: it is what in oneself appears to be the experience of bliss, and is therefore realised in oneself.

Vasishta later goes on to say about the illusory nature of the world:

This Maya (world appearance) will continue to flow with ever-changing appearance until the truth is realised, and only then will maya cease to operate. Wherever this Maya functions in whatever manner, remember it is only because of the existence of the ego sense. Immediately (when) the truth concerning the ego sense is investigated and understood, this Maya vanishes.

The problem is that we have identified with the manifested *Maya* and taken it as real rather than identified with our own Divinity. Over time, our Divinity has become increasingly hazy and muddy, through our excursions in and out of different bodies and lives, situations and experiences. In time the *I* we are consciously aware of (the ego-self) with its many garments, forgets who it really is. It thinks that the garment it is wearing is who it really is!

The Dirty Old Coat

A beautiful woman wears a gift she has received of an attractive coat. She likes to wear it always and, in the course of time, the coat becomes faded and dirty. Some holes and tears appear on the material as well as some stains and muddy patches. The coat does not even fit her anymore but still she has become attached to it and does not want to take it off. She feels safe and protected wearing the coat. She even begins to think that it brings her good luck.

The woman now looks like an old tramp and her true attractiveness is hidden. She gets so accustomed and attached to this coat that she dies in it without ever knowing how beautiful she really was. In fact, she completely forgot about herself and in the end identified with herself as the dirty old coat. She was so attached to this old coat, that she was reborn some months later wearing the same coat and the whole drama repeated itself until she finally managed to take the coat off. She had not realised just how shining and radiant she was !

In the same way, we forget our Source, That which we truly are, and if we think of it at all, it is like a fairytale, rather than our reality. At some point in the drama we become entirely lost. From then on our healing is a journey of unconscious pilgrimage through different bodies until we re-discover our perfect and Whole Self—when we take off our dirty and worn out old coats!

Your journey of *rediscovery* involves learning how to live comfortably with yourself for some time *along* with the old coat you have acquired. That is, until you are fully ready to take it off. I say this because you cannot take off your coat until you are ready. You have been wearing it a long time. Most probably, it would be too overwhelming to even consider the idea. So, why give yourself any more unnecessary suffering?

All you need to do is become increasingly aware of this dilemma with compassion towards yourself and others and with non-judgement. Have compassion because imagine how uncomfortable it really is to be wearing these old coats. When you begin to understand how you have been treating yourself and others, this awareness alone will **HEAL** you and help you towards your goal.

With some of the practical ideas in this section, you will, in your own time, gain the confidence to take your old coat off and see who you really are and what you truly look like. You will know, through the increasing awareness of your heart, when and how to discard it. Your ego will never want to sacrifice this covering because it gives your ego an identity and something to cling to. But your Heart will know the truth and at the right time, with Divine compassion, will release you.

What a shock is in store for your poor little ego. Imagine how it feels at the possibility of being stripped naked, not to be able to have its comfort blanket—made from the old, worn-out persona coat. No wonder your ego tries with everything it has learned over aeons, to control you and fool you, to dissuade you, and even terrify you into remaining as you are.

But the Heart knows how to reassure that destitute little scrap of an ego. It knows how to lighten it up and play with it. It teaches the ego not to be so serious and to loosen up and experiment. Maybe there is a role for the ego after all, the ego thinks—maybe I can play without being too attached. Perhaps I can just slip one arm out of my coat and see what it feels like.

Your dirty, old coat is your idea of what you think you are—what are, to you, your precious thoughts, feelings, attitudes, emotions and accompanying desires and attachments. They are your almost concrete patterns of behaviour, which determine your choices in life and which create your life's journey and experience. But they are *Not You*! That is all you need to remember in this coming tug-of-war between your ego and your True Self. Even the most down trodden tramp would not want to be seen dead in the coat. Your ego, on the other hand, will grasp onto this old coat as if it is in the face of grim death, no matter what the price, until it can relax, feel safe and let go. It will do this, no matter how tight, how loose or how positively painful it is to wear this garment.

So, against all the seeming odds, you will one day be able to take that dirty coat off and find your real beauty and grace. You are already on the way, even if you think you are not. Everything and everyone is on its way towards rejoining its Source, God, towards the realisation of its Truth. In this lifetime, you will either *progress* towards this Wholeness, or you will be That Wholeness before you leave the body you are now in. You will merge with Divinity.

In this part of the book, there are some practical remedies, tonics and medicines to help you towards your cure. As you are healing towards your Wholeness, you will find that you will be sad, happy, frustrated, in love, alone, fulfilled and peaceful, as well as a myriad of other emotions and feelings. None of these feeling can stop you, and remember that none of them are *IT*. Just use whatever methods you feel drawn to, explore and have a commitment to stay with the process.

Eventually everything you have will have to be discarded. Nothing lasts. Nothing can last in this temporal world of ours—even if, in a rare case, you find a satisfaction of a desire to last for many years. For example, you might be one half of a lucky couple who really has found your *soul mate*. Nevertheless, you and your soul mate will have to die and move on some day! Usually, one of you will go before the other and one of you will be left. When you both leave your body, it is not certain that you will be together again. As you identify yourself with your body, senses and feelings you are merely a temporary form of cosmic power. But, when you let this identification with the temporary go, you will find that you are Cosmic Power Itself.

At the same time, remember that none of your experiences can be a waste. Appreciate all that you experience as a means towards your discovery. Everything and everyone is a spark of God. How, therefore, can any experience, any spark of God, be a waste? These are all part of your growing. As you continue towards your Wholeness, you will at times enjoy a respite or a remission and you may feel terrific, Truly welcome this. These are high opportunities of well being, of hints of your Wholeness even if they are not *It*. They are like large spoonfuls of Grace, which give you the boost and the energy to tackle further the real work. With discrimination you can use this time and energy well. What is important, is that you do not stop.

As you **HEAL**, you will discover that although all of your desirous and sensory feelings have nothing much to do with *you* at all, you will find the greatest compassion and tenderness for the you who experiences them and for everyone else who is caught by them. We all deserve this compassion and forgiveness. With these feelings, emotions and attitudes we have, we do not know any better. We hurt. Remember this and always be kind to yourself and others as you discover your mutual vulnerabilities.

We are all beautiful, even when we are a little lost, disoriented and temporary Cosmic human forms. We are all in the same boat wearing our old coats. We are each struggling with the same dreams and nightmares and are desperate for healing. We need to cultivate understanding and consideration for these aspects in ourselves and in others, which need to have their comfort blankets and which will finally have to let go of them to the Unknown. Reassure them, console yourself that, as you paddle your boat to God, none of us can be destroyed. Only the Maya can be dissolved.

Everything, you, your journey through all your lives, were created by your Cosmic Self. Remember this and you will find sustenance until you complete your journey back to the Beginning, to your Cure, to God.

You are Wholeness.
You are Love.
You will know yourself as God.
This is the Cure.

HEAL

The Dream

11

When you sleep, you have dreams in which you experience joys and sorrows.
They seem real as long as you are dreaming.
On waking, you realise that they were all unreal and mere dreams.
In the waking state you have other experiences.
What is the relationship between these two categories of experiences?
What you experience in the waking state is also a dream: a waking dream!
The reality is that in both the states—
the sleeping and the waking—you are present as the dreamer !

Sri Sathya Sai Baba

What is a dream and how can it be helpful to you? How can it help you to take off that old coat? Is a dream something that happens merely to us when we are sleeping and which we sometimes remember or forget, or is it something that is happening also when we think we are awake? Is a dream simply the mind's way of releasing itself of stored feelings and thoughts, or can it be looked at as something more profound than this? Can it be a way of understanding what our very Divinity is saying to us?

Whether we are awake or asleep, a dream is an experience of our mind. It is an answer to all of the above questions. It can be an expression and release of suppressed feelings and emotions. But it is also a healing tool of our minds. Through my years of training in Dreamwork and working with my own and other people's dreams I am convinced that the dream is also a key to revealing the radiance which is underneath our old coats.

At the very least, the dream releases within us deep repressed or uncomfortable feelings and this allows us to be more emotionally relaxed. But we can also look at what the evocative symbols and imagery represent; we can examine what our subconscious mind is saying to us. We can grasp more of the Wholeness of ourselves—what is truly motivating us and making us live out our lives in the ways that we are and what is behind this Maya.

When we wake up from a dream, we may have palpitations or discover that we are sweating. We may be aware of emotions like fear or anxiety or have happy feelings. If the dream we have had has been particularly vivid and provocative, the feelings we experience may be with us for some time through the day until their impact begins to fade a little. Clearly, though, and very importantly, no matter how vivid the dream and how much it affected us, we are aware of waking up from it and of having more detachment to it than when we were dreaming it.

Because we can wake up, and be more detached from the dream we may even be able to laugh at it, though it was a nightmare. For, how can we take something not real so seriously? If we watch a movie on TV and it is sad or has a sad ending, do we then spend the rest of our lives being unhappy because of it? If we did this it would be crazy of us and other people would definitely laugh at us.

Importantly, in the same way we can also see our day experiences as a dream. Just as we have the ability to wake up from our experiences of the night dream and discover that it was not real, we can do the same with our day experiences. Just as the night experiences can disappear when we awake, so can the day experiences evaporate. Even though our bodies may still experience some physiological effects of either the night or day stories, we can be much more detached about what is happening to us day or night—no matter how relieved or disappointed we are when we wake up from the dreams.

When I get caught in taking my day experiences as very real, I try to remember about happenings years before. I try to think of scenes in which I was very affected, and which I thought I would never recover from. Sometimes when I do this I can hardly relate to what happened at all. The whole memory is so vague, like a nebulous dream. I am so different now to the person who experienced this that it seems like another lifetime. Everything feels so distant and irrelevant looking from the perspective of now. This realisation helps me to know that everything I feel, am encountering now, no matter how seemingly important, will be just as misty and of so little importance one day.

So, the fact is we can say to ourselves that everything is really just a story, and all that we are going through is really ***only a dream***. And here, as far as I am concerned, contains the most important message of dreams. Here is the jewel. However, even though a story, I still feel gratitude for the day and night dreams, as they are incidents and states of mind which are a part of my journey towards Wholeness.

Dreamwork

Systems for Dreamwork are found, for example, in Buddhism, Taoism and Hinduism. In almost every indigenous culture there are a wealth of dream symbols, imagery and ways of understanding dreams. The dream as a means of receiving Divine communication, to our knowledge, is as ancient as records permit. Mamu for example was honoured as the Babylonian Goddess of dreams, approximately 5000 years before Christ.

One of the most famous dream interpreters was, of course, Joseph in the Old Testament, although throughout the Old and the New Testament of the Bible, there are various references to dreams, and how they are recognised as ways in which God spoke to the people.

Dreams, as predictive tools were also considered serious enough for Joseph's jealous brothers to hate him and throw him in the well because of the information of his coming greatness that he received in his dreams. He told them, *Listen to this dream that I dreamed. There we were, binding sheaves in the field. Suddenly my sheaf rose and stood upright; then your sheaves gathered around it, and bowed down to my sheaf.*

Even his beloved father rebuked him when he said of another dream, *the sun, the moon and eleven stars were bowing down to me.*

But even though Joseph's brothers conspired to kill him, it was not God's will, and they were unable to prevent his dreams from coming true. His dreams were the message from Divinity Itself.

For as long as they remember, the Australian Aborigines call the spiritual dimensions they connect to, the *Dreamtime*—where they believe that the different levels of beings and dimensions are found. Another tribal consciousness that became famous in the 1970s for their inclusion of dreams and Dreamwork as an integral part of social life, is that of the Senoi, hunting and gathering tribe from Malaysia.

Kilton Stewart first introduced the ways of the Senoi to the West. He described them as a culture free from mental and physical diseases. Each morning, they met to share their dream experiences. They had sophisticated techniques of dream control, such as making their dreams have positive outcomes. They believed in the power of the dream symbols, so much so that they creatively reproduced them in various art forms. They believed that each symbol had been given to them as a healing gift from the dream.

My own professional background in dreams is Jungian-Senoi, with Strephon Kaplan Williams, in Mandala Dreamwork Training and with the Jungian psychoanalyst, Bani Shorter, as well as Tibetan Buddhist and Hindu practitioners. My first training in Dreamwork was Mandala Dreamwork. This was a combination of Jungian and Senoi principles and was highly creative. A small group of us studied for two to three years in Scotland with Strephon Kaplan Williams and Hilary Scaife, and then began leading Dream Groups. Later, I worked with Bani Shorter, for more than two years during which time I learned about the wealth of the unconscious mind, the archetypes and the language of symbols as healing tools. Jung was one of the first in the field of Psychology to identify the unity of symbolic language in the Collective Unconscious as well as universal aspects of The Self, such as The Shadow.

But, because of my earlier out-of-body Astral Realm experiences, I felt I had to extend my interest further than the psychological. Therefore, I later researched some techniques of Dream Yoga and received instructions and transmissions on the Bardo Teachings, (the Tibetan Buddhist teachings on journeying through the different stages of dying and the after life up to rebirth). My Tibetan Buddhist teachers and my Hindu Advaita teachers have enabled me to understand how to use the concept of dreams to discover the illusory nature of both states of reality, the night dream and the day dream, as a means to wake up to the Truth of the Self.

I continue to teach Dreamwork and to lead Dream Groups using the skills I learned from the Jungian and Senoi traditions, but I now include the concept of the Bardo as a means of taking people further towards Wholeness. The word Bardo means the intermediate state between death and rebirth, but these states occur continuously throughout life and death. In working with our dreams, we can learn how to see those moments of transition and there is the possibility to wake up.

Enlightened Masters throughout the ages tell us that our day reality is as much a dream as a night dream. They explain that one day we will wake up from the illusion of life and death and know its *unreality*—that is has only been a story of the mind.

Tibetan Buddhism offers an entire spiritual training and practice in Dream Yoga, called the Practice of the Night. Tibetan culture values dreams and Dreamwork. There is a class of dreams called *Milan Ter—Dream Treasures,* the teachings of Enlightened Beings, which are often rediscovered in dreams. However, the dream offers more than this even. Here there is the possibility of developing awareness within the dream-state and of learning how to control dreams. In the course of a typical night, we may sleep anything between six to eight hours. In sleep, there is a large portion of our life, that if we remain unconscious to it, we will know nothing about. The following Buddhist prayer tells us:

When the state of dreaming has dawned,
do not lie in ignorance like a corpse.
Enter the natural sphere of unwavering attentiveness.
Recognise your dreams and transform illusion into luminosity.

Do not sleep like an animal.
Do the practice which mixes sleep and reality.

Namkhai Norbu—
Dream Yoga and The Practice of Natural Light

The lucidity that can be learnt through making more conscious the dream experiences of the night are, of course, of tremendous value when applied to the lucid awareness of after-death states. The preparation for this is also a lucidity of awareness in our day states. And, we can be awake in either realm and be a conscious witness to the events, rather than be an unconscious victim of them.

Perhaps you have had an experience in a night dream where you realise that you are dreaming, but you have let the dream go on and even directed the sequences of events. If you have discovered this skill, you can also practice this with the happenings of your day reality too. Be happy, for you are well on your way to understanding the possibilities of dream awareness assisting you towards Wholeness. Even if you have not had this experience, be open to the possibility of it, and you will increasingly find the opportunities to allow it to happen.

In both realities, there is actually very little difference between the two types of dreams. The two levels of relative reality are *stories or enactments* that the mind wants to play out within the context of certain situations, experiences and roles. From the vantage of the witnesser, each can reveal highly symbolic and meaningful insights as to how we are bound and caught by our internal unconscious and subconscious minds. They reveal to us our old coats and how we are wearing them.

In the following examples of how to look at your dreams, play with the dream experiences of both the night and so-called day reality. If you are going for Wholeness it is not enough just to consider night dreams. You are dreaming now even as you read this—the only difference is that you appeared to wake up this morning from a different kind of sleep, and you moved into another kind of reality (which is actually another kind of sleep). It is just that your mind is

now identified with this *waking ego* and it seems to be more conscious than the one it may remember from your sleep!

You can wake up more and more by cultivating this awareness and you will find that you become increasingly detached from your *dreaming*. The more you become acquainted with viewing in this witnessing way, the more you will be able to discriminate between the real and the unreal. Cultivate the onlooker in you to be your mediator in this duality, until you can wake up from your movie.

So How Do We Begin ?

Keep a journal by your bedside.
Write down dreams as you remember them.
Everyone dreams every night even though they may not remember.
As soon as you are willing to remember dreams, the mind
has a knack of letting them surface to your more conscious mind.

If you do not recall any night dreams,
concentrate on the experiences of the day.
These are also dreams.
Take some time each day or each week,
choose a theme or a happening,
write the events in your journal.

In this way you can work with either or both night and day dreams. Doing one is not really any better than doing the other, but they do complement each other. The understanding of the night dream may, for example, give you a deeper insight into the more unconscious and hidden reasons you have for acting out the outer daydream in the way that you do.

Steps to Help You Wake Up

Continually ask questions.
Never be satisfied with the surface answers.
For example,
choose a recent night or day-dream scenario that has a
powerful affect on you,

one that disturbs you,
challenges you,
that has an effect on you emotionally, mentally or spiritually,
or one that is lucid and which you cannot easily forget.

Write down the details of the event in as much a
detached and clear way as possible.
Try to keep your emotions out of it at this time.
Concentrate only on the details.
For example,
if your dream began by you walking along a dark street at 10 p.m.
write this down.
Write down the whole event as you remember it in this way,
as though you are an investigative journalist.

Itemise the details in number and line form rather than
writing in long paragraphs.
Our psyches get lost in long, elaborate descriptions.

Write down what you, the day or night-dream self is doing.

For example,
I am walking along the street.
I am aware that it is dark.
I am aware of looking upwards.
I am aware of looking sideways to see if there is light anywhere.
I am aware that it is misty.
I am aware that my feet are wet.
I am wearing old leather shoes.
I see a woman wearing a dirty old coat.

Now write down what your dream self is not doing.

For example,
I am not looking at the sky.
I am not looking for any people.
I am not aware of what I am wearing.

I am not aware of what I am feeling.
I ignore the woman wearing the old coat.
I am not looking where I am going.

Now write down what your dream self is feeling or not feeling.

For example,
As I walk down the street I feel afraid at the traffic lights.
I feel uneasy when I realise that I am in the dark.
I feel nothing as I look for the light.
I feel afraid of the woman with the old coat on.
I do not like my shoes.

Dream Symbols

Take a note of the symbols of the dream,
the ones that affect you more than others,
these can be any object or person in your dream.
Everything in the dream is a symbol.
Whatever the symbol, it can only be understood fully and truly by you.
Everything in the dream is YOU.

For example,
A woman wearing a dirty old coat.
A traffic light at the colour green.
A damp pavement.
Darkness.
Light.
Old leather shoes.

Ask the question,

What does this symbol mean to me?
What does a woman wearing an old dirty coat mean to me?
How is the woman an aspect of me?
How do the shoes represent my life right now?

What does a traffic light at green tell me about my life at the moment?
Do these symbols tell me I am comfortable at the moment?
What would I like to do with any of the symbols now?

Now read and contemplate on what you have written and found.

Some further questions you can ask.

What is the dream saying to me about how I am feeling?
What attitudes or assumptions do I hold that the dream is showing me?
How valid are my feelings in the dream?
What are these feelings based on?
Do they have anything to do with what is actually happening to me while awake?
What is actually happening to me in the dream?
What am I really doing?
What feelings am I having now as I remember the dream?
Who/what do I not like in the dream and why?
How would I like to change the dream?

When you feel that you understand the dream more, change the dream in any way you wish to.

Re-write

the outcome of the dream,
the circumstances,
anything you wish to.

As an act of healing,

re-write the whole scene, as you would like it to happen now.
Re-write your role in it as you would like it to be now.
Re-write the script.

Offer your new script as a prayer for your healing to God.

Something like,
Dear Lord,

I offer you this request for a new script
for healing,
acceptance,
peace,
and for the good of all concerned.

Finally

Trust.
Let the whole situation rest for a little while and relax.
Re-read your writing some time later, as though reading a story.
You will realise that it was a story.
You will know that it was all a dream.

The castles and towers you see in dreams,
melt into nothing when you open your eyes.
No lamp can glow brightly in daylight.
Night alone can reveal its value.

HEAL

The following is an excerpt from the ancient text, *The Quintessential Instructions of Mind* found in—*Dream Yoga and the Practice of Natural Light* by Namkhai Norbu:

The Buddha No Further Than One's Palm

What will be obtained by grasping after a mirage?
What is the purpose of following after these varied dreams?
To what benefit is grasping onto space?
By various concepts one turns one's own head around.
Put aside this exhausting meaninglessness and relax into
the primordial sphere.
The real sky is (knowing) that samsara and nirvana are
merely an illusory display.
Although there are multifarious displays, view them with one taste.

(By being) intimate with meditation one can immediately recollect sky-like awareness...

Dream Teachings

I wrote in the last chapter of how I experienced teachings during out-of-body episodes while I was awake. But this can also happen during night dreams. I have had many such experiences, and particularly from my Guru. Sri Sathya Sai Baba says that no one can dream of Him unless He wills it. I know of many other people who also have had dreams where their Gurus, embodied spiritual teachers, as well as out-of-body spiritual teachers have instructed them in their dreams.

The following is the first dream I heard about involving Sai Baba, and a devotee of His in 1990 relayed it to me. I had only briefly heard of Sai Baba at that time and had no idea how important He was going to be in my life.

A participant in one of the weekly Dream Groups I was leading in the UK told the account of the Sai Baba dream to me. Sylvia brought the dream to share with the group as part of our weekly work. As I heard the dream, I was aware that there was little I could say about it to her in the usual psychological way. The dream was *Divine and had a Divine message.* It followed a visit Sylvia made to see Sai Baba in Puttapurti in 1987.

The Dream of the Beloved Who Lovingly Grants Us Our Wishes

Sylvia related:

I am walking along a riverbank and on my left side I am about to pass an old- fashioned riverboat (with big wooden paddles). I decide to go up the gangway and I find an audience ready for some performance. I sit down. Further up the aisle, I see Sai Baba walking up the centre. He stops to talk to an Indian lady who is sitting two rows behind me.

I am acutely aware of Him and I think, "What a lucky woman to have Him talk to her." Yet I am aware that He knows what I am thinking. After a while He passes me and beckons me with His hand to follow Him. I do this and follow Him to a room behind the stage, which is all decked out for a large dinner party, resplendent with shining silver cutlery and crystal glass and beautiful flower arrangements.

We stand at the top end of the table where there are two place settings and chairs and I am given to understand that these seats are for Him and me. He points out His arm towards the table and says, "This is all for you!"

I am dumbfounded and wake up in a state of bliss. I cannot believe what He has just said. There were as yet no other guests at the table. The room was empty but for Him and myself.

Sylvia told me how she had sometimes felt that she was not good enough for God, or undeserving of God's Grace and Love. This dream was therefore a tremendous loving healing of this feeling she had. Here, Sai Baba showed her that she, too, is special and cherished by God. The river is symbolic of the river of life and the boat, her journey, her means to God. In the dream, Sai Baba, Who is God in Form for her, reveals to her how He loves her.

Some years later, I myself began visiting Sai Baba, and on my third visit was in Prashanti Nilayam in 1997 at the time of Mahashivaratri, the annual festival of Lord Shiva, the Destroyer of illusion. On this visit I stayed for three weeks. During Darshan time and particularly as Swami passed me I sometimes saw Sylvia's face in my mind or thought about her. It was as though Sai Baba was reminding me of Sylvia each time He passed me. I wondered why this was happening—if it was because Sylvia was the first person to ever talk about Sai Baba to me. In those days, she was also the only person I knew who had visited Sai Baba. She had later become a dear friend, and so I supposed that it was quite natural for me to remember her. But there did seem more to it, as the experience was so strong and I knew that everything Sai Baba does with us must have a deep meaning.

I was living in India now, and had not seen Sylvia for some time, and as I was writing to a mutual friend, I asked how Sylvia was and whether she was all right. The friend faxed me shortly afterwards to say that Sylvia was not well at all, and that breast cancer had recently been discovered. She was to have an operation.

Before I left Prashanti Nilayam and before I knew about Sylvia's condition, Swami not only personally manifested *vibhutti* (sacred ash with miraculous healing powers) for me but at my request, He also blessed some for me to give to people in need. One of the people I had in mind was Sylvia.

Sai Baba says about the giving of *vibhutti*:

When vibhutti is given, Swami wants the recipient to understand this Advaitam, (Basic Oneness). The devotee should get rid of Ahamkara (ego arising from the feeling of separateness) and sense of Mamakara ("mine" and "thine"). These two are based on name and form and when they are destroyed, the underlying unity of the Divine can be realised.

Time and events had passed since Sylvia first visited Sai Baba. She never forgot Him, although He was not always uppermost in her mind now. Even so, she had asked me some time before to try to get her some *vibhutti* if I visited Sai Baba, as she had run out of her supply from her visit all those years ago. I was able to send her some of this *vibhutti,* personally blessed by Sai Baba at her time of need.

I was in no doubt that Sai Baba had reached out to Sylvia during this critical time, and this was one of the ways He wished to show His Love to her. I saw how the Love of a Guru really does not let go or forget us, even when the Guru might not be uppermost in our thoughts. By His continual reminding me of Sylvia, each time He passed me, Sai Baba showed me that He knew that she was ill. Not only that, He blessed *vibhutti* so that I could send some on to her.

His Love was later confirmed by what also happened to Sylvia around the same time in the UK. She had recently moved to England from Scotland to be nearer her family. Although she was happy to be with her family, she felt a little alienated from like-minded friends.

Just before she was to go into Hospital for her operation, Sai Baba devotees in the area contacted her unexpectedly. Through a series of seeming coincidences, they had received her new address and she began to attend weekly Sai Baba meetings, where His teachings are studied and discussed and where spiritual songs, *bhajans*, are sung. Interestingly, the people who instigated this were the very ones with whom she travelled to India to see Sai Baba 10 years before. Her Sai Baba friends were also able to support her and help her through the testing time of her operation and treatment.

Later, in 1999, although Sylvia had never thought that she would return to India, she visited my husband Sudevan and me in Kerala and we travelled together to visit Sai Baba. Her cancer had gone and she was cured. As Swami sometimes says to people He has cured, "*Cancer cancelled!*"

As Swami passed us one afternoon after *bhajan* singing, He looked at her giving her the most tremendous and joyous smile. She felt in bliss—saying, *Now I can say God smiled at me.*

I am aware of a golden thread of Divine Love weaving its way through these events that spanned more than 10 years. The encounter, the dream, the visits, the discovery and the healing all feel as one profound teaching—that God is always present with us. Here Divinity used the day and night dream experiences to give God's reassuring message of Love and Compassion. God was and is always there for Sylvia and for everyone. We are God's special guests in the banquet of Life and will always be cherished.

Using a Journal

12

According to my experience, it is clear that if each individual makes an effort then he or she can change. Of course, change is not immediate and it takes a lot of time. In order to change and deal with emotions it is crucial to analyse which thoughts are useful, constructive and of benefit to us. I mean mainly those thoughts which make us calmer, more relaxed and which give us peace of mind, versus those thoughts, which create uneasiness, fear and frustration.

The Dalai Lama—***The Dalai Lama's Book of Wisdom***

It is healing to be able to express your feelings as they arise. In this way you can know what your emotions are and how they are prompting you in every little thing you do and say. On the journey towards Wholeness, you will have many feelings and emotions rise to the surface like the waves of a turbulent sea—just as these waves surge and then subside, your emotions and feelings will rise and fall. Everything changes with time. Even if you try with all your heart to retain a feeling, an emotion, you will be unable to do so. Still, they will profoundly affect you. You can purify your emotions more deeply and quickly if you can feel them appropriately. *To feel is to HEAL.*

The fact that emotions change tells you something about the fickleness of your feelings. In this case how can you trust them enough to follow them so blindly as you do? But, that is another story. In the meantime, what can you do with them as they arise? One of the healing tools you can use is a journal.

For the moment, you need to find a way to appropriately express your feelings so that they are not repressed or hurtful to yourself and others. If you do not know how to do this, your feelings will explode, when you least expect them to. Or you will just inwardly fume with your unexpressed rage, for example. You are only human and ignited by that fire, you will lash out at others, strangers sometimes. But, most likely, closest and dearest loved ones will be your victims.

If you are able to express fully what you feel as quickly as you can after feeling it, then that feeling has the opportunity to change immediately. Doing this, you change also and transform and grow from the experience of allowing the feeling to be expressed. A feeling is just what it says it is. It is something to be felt. It is not something to be held onto and allowed to rule you. It is not sacrosanct. It is a temporary, relative sense experience !

When you express your feelings, your emotional body will be like a pond that has been stirred up, with silt coming to the surface, cleaned and then allowed to become calm again. Silt will still most probably be at the bottom of your emotional body, just like in the pond, but, you will have allowed more of the surface dirt to be cleaned and, eventually, all the silt can be cleared in this way.

As mentioned, Jung used the concept of *The Shadow*. Because The Shadow holds within the psyche all that is repressed, unacceptable, unknown and denied—that which you dis-identify with, it becomes the pool of your projections. In looking at what is reflected in your external world, you have an ideal mirror for seeing and making conscious all that is hidden within you. How many times have you reacted strongly to someone else's foibles only to discover that they really mirror a great fear within you? Perhaps you sense that you have similar tendencies, and seeing these exaggerated in another person will trigger your fear. You will know when this is happening because your ego will feel threatened and you may, for example, feel hostile or aggressive, angry or defensive. Does this sound familiar ?

Repressed feelings are part and parcel of this shady baggage! People are often completely surprised by what is revealed when they allow what is in The Shadow to more consciously manifest. But it must be done, otherwise you will stay very unconscious. One way to become aware of what is hidden in your Shadow is to allow the space, the opening or arena for it.

I found that when people first came to Dream Groups or entered psychotherapy and space was created for the expression of their unconscious, a wealth of material arose in them and became available for clarity and healing. The unconscious and subconscious minds are full of life longing to be expressed. We are like full treasure chests, locked up, and we need to be given the opportunity to *open up, unload and shine.*

Sometimes, these aspects of us have been so buried that we initially do not even identify with what they are. Although we will never completely know ourselves, likewise how can we know the entire ocean? We may not ever be able to trust ourselves in relation to the mind (and its thoughts). But, we can make a commitment to explore the mind and we can do this through the keeping of a simple journal.

To daily write, for say 20 minutes, in a journal is one way of making a commitment to your psyche (the mind). Here, you allow the space for your psyche to develop and be creative. The more it has this freedom, the more it will be able to play itself out. The more it can play out in every imaginable game it wishes to, in an appropriate setting, the more you will be freed from its bondage.

Patients usually think that they have a fairly good idea of why they go into therapy but, frequently, what they discover is not what they could ever have imagined. I have worked with people, for example, who had no idea that they were abused as children until they came for counselling. Maybe they had some problem at work, and they came to talk it over in a few sessions. But, that therapeutic hour gave the psyche space to open its Pandora's Box. In that opening, they found memories coming to the surface of childhood abuse or some other experiences which they had completely gone to sleep on and had seemingly forgotten in their conscious minds and lives.

It is often the same when people commit to a spiritual path. To begin with, everything is *light and love,* and many think that they have found heaven… But, when the work becomes deeper, the meditations and prayers get stronger—the prayers are answered and the purifying starts to happen, many people just do not know what has hit them!

Ignorance Is Bliss

I remember hearing how a Tibetan Buddhist Rinpoche said to a friend not to worry if she was feeling and looking so terrible on the spiritual retreat she was on. She found herself surrounded by people on the retreat who were saying that they were feeling terrific and who were looking great. Rinpoche happily told her,

"Don't worry, the methods are working on you because you look so bad."

This is the last thing most people would choose to have happen to them. There are many people who, if they knew what they would go through entering the spiritual path, would run miles from any open doorway leading to the Light! In these cases, ignorance is initially the only bliss you are going to get.

I had a similar experience after I went on my first pilgrimage in India in 1993.

Better to Die!

I travelled from Sikkim with an old ani (nun) in her 80s who was an auntie of the Rinpoche I had been staying with and receiving teachings from. Though she was in her 80s she was stronger and hardier than I was. I learned a great deal from her and our pilgrimage together. We also travelled with Rinpoche's cousin, a young monk who had recently come from Tibet. We were like three innocent babes in the worldly wood. We began in Sikkim and by train and bus travelled to the plains of India, to Sarnath, Varanasi and Bodhgaya in Bihar—where Buddha gave His first teachings and where He became Enlightened under the Bodhi Tree.

Physically, it was a long and gruelling journey but the spiritual experiences were worth it. While in Bodhgaya, I had a profound experience of bliss that lasted for many days. When I contracted, however, after the expansion, I developed a fever that almost killed me. It happened immediately as the bus drove away from Bodhgaya and continued while we travelled back to Darjeeling on an 18-hour journey.

It took me almost two years to recover from the physical and psychic affects of the expansion/contraction and I had to receive treatment from Tibetan doctors to strengthen again my shattered nervous system. When I first told Rinpoche what had happened to me however, he said, rather sadly,

"It is a pity you only got sick—it would have been much better, if you had died. "

He then beamed a huge smile at my reaction. He was teasing me, but Rinpoche was also telling me that the best thing that can happen to a pilgrim is that he or she die on a pilgrimage.

In retrospect, I am sure that this means also, the death of my ego and not only physically. Rinpoche's brutally stark remark brought home to me the essential purpose of my spiritual path and pilgrimage—and what I had got into…

Your Pandora's Box gets full, and when it does, something has to give. Say you have a meeting with someone, and because they do something you don't like, you feel hurt. Maybe this person didn't do much, but the action triggered something in you that was already hurt and which you had never been able to release. Imagine what you might do in this kind of circumstance? At the very worst, you might want to commit murder, and at the very least you may respond with a scathing remark that will end possible further good relations with that person.

Perhaps you will withdraw and cut that person out of your life forever and forget about it until someone else does the same thing again, and so you repeat the pattern. It is these kinds of scenarios that often happen when husbands and wives, relatives and friends stop speaking to each other and become enemies instead. How many times do you really need to put yourself through this kind of suffering?

There is no doubt that if you do, you will continue riding the painful cycle of *Samsara.* Sai Baba defines this as *the movement into one form after another.*

And Sai Baba says:

Today we sow the seed of thought-karma and reap the fruit of action. From the seed of karma arises svabhaava (the fruit of behaviour). Out of the seed of behaviour comes the fruit of character. The seed of character yields the fruit of Adhrishtam (fortune). Thus, from thought to fortune, the chain of human progress can be perceived. Our good and bad luck is thus linked to our thoughts. The mind immerses man in impenetrable darkness through bad thoughts. The same mind can lift man to sublime heights by good thoughts. Thus, thoughts are supremely important for man. They constitute his life-breath. Without understanding this truth, man allows his evil tendencies like anger, envy, hatred and conceit to fill his mind and thereby court disaster

And this is where journal writing can be so helpful. You journal is a *friend* that you can off-load to. When you release your feelings, you can balance your thoughts and emotions more and you can identify those that will continue to cause you pain and those which are helpful to you.

It is not always appropriate to say something back in response to an unkind remark from another. It may be appropriate to say something at the time, but then again, it may not. When you express your feelings in a safe and contained way, as in a journal, you can begin to understand what your hurt has to do with someone else's remark. It is your hurt. Someone else, in the same circumstances as you, may feel nothing, or worse.

Your hurt is, therefore, something personally to do with you. You need to be a mother to that hurt and do what can be done to HEAL the wound completely so that it stops bleeding and draining you. Most of the pain you feel will have very little to do with the recent hurting event. This event has triggered you to feel the wound already there. How can it be of any help to pull this trigger on someone, something that had nothing much to do with your hurt in the first place? The cause of your hurt is more easily recognised when seen in black and white on a piece of paper.

Writing in Your Journal

Begin by writing and not thinking of what to write.
If you want to write about a situation, write how you feel about it.
Reassure and contain your psyche by limiting the writing period.
Do not go over this limit.
The containment allows your conscious, unconscious
and subconscious mind to relax and feel held enough by you to let go.
Do not be too concerned about reading what you have written.
You can do this later.
If you feel stuck,
write down some basic questions to yourself.
If you are right-handed, write with your left hand or vice versa.

Helpful Questions You Can Ask Yourself

What/who does this situation/person remind me of?
Did he/she feel more like my mother or my father talking to me?
What age do I feel right now?
What would I have really liked to say to him/her?
What is my dirty old coat like?
How comfortable do I feel wearing it?
If this coat could speak to me, what would it say?
Have a dialogue with your coat,
or with any person or object in the dream.
Or
be the object or person and express what he/she/it wants to say.

HEAL

It is important to try not to rush the exercise. But it also important not to frighten or bore your psyche by writing for hours until, say, you get the answer. Actually, what is a right answer? What matters is allowing the space for the expression and discovering whatever it is. Depending on the degree of hurt and emotional material that you are holding, relative to a particular theme, it is likely you will need to spend some time over many different sessions. When you do this and you begin to feel *empty,* free, or released, or can even laugh at yourself or the incident, you will know that you have begun to HEAL towards Wholeness.

When you feel release in this way, you are likely to experience a burst of energy within a few days. I often say, *It takes a lot of energy to hold energy down.* When you are freed of the holding and pressing down on your psyche you can feel much lighter and fantastic. You are more *emptied*, more grounded in reality and you are less on the seesaw of emotional life.

Verily you are suspended like scales between your sorrow and your joy.
Only when you are empty are you at standstill and balanced.
When the treasure-keeper lifts you to weigh his gold and his silver,
needs must your joy or your sorrow rise or fall.

Kahil Gibran—*The Prophet*

Similarly, when you use so much of your precious life to keep down what you want to remain hidden or neatly tucked away, there is a bound to be a reaction at some point—this is the stuff that implodes and causes chronic illness and pain and an acute healing crisis to arise. But when true inner healing takes place, there is always a feeling of an increase of vitality and additional *Prana* (life force) available to you. This is a clear indication of the validity of the release.

What about If It Feels Too Much to Feel?

Stop for a while and relax with the feeling.
Let the tears come.
Crying is a healing gift.
If there are angry feelings allow them to be.

When you can, peek beneath the anger and find the hurt.
Sip some cool water
or
have a cup of tea.
Do something that makes you feel happy.
Congratulate yourself and tell yourself that you are doing well.

HEAL

Making Conscious Relationships

Unexpressed hurts are the main cause of the breakdown of intimate relationships. When we are very close to someone our feelings can be highly evoked/provoked in relationship to the *other.* The closer the relationship the more evoked, provoked and intense our feelings might be. Most of what is stirred up in us will be feelings we experienced from our earliest intimate relationships, and then we project these past pains onto our present partners and those closest to us. In this way, we live out recurrent psychic themes until we eventually can understand what we are doing and let go of them and **HEAL.**

How we experienced and understood our mother and father, for example, had an indelible imprinting on us which will have a lot to do with how we will experience later relationships. We constantly project these initial imprints onto future others who sometimes do not even remotely resemble our parents or early care givers in any psychic way.

How we feel life relates to us and everyone in it, is also a reflection of the way we feel about God. This is our primordial relationship! If we feel abused, we think that God abuses us and will continue to abuse us. If we think that God will abuse us, then we will look to be abused by life. It is a frightening circle of cause and effect. I have met many people who expect to be *punished* by God.

But, how you experienced your childhood has a lot to do with how you lived, related and died in your previous lives. You are the result of this imprinting and colouring. This is why everyone is so individual in his/her pain and growth, and why there is no *one right way for all.* This need not be an overwhelming concept, however. You are now the sum total of everything and everyone you have been.

When you make the commitment to **HEAL**, you **HEAL** your history. I have also been taught by Shamans who told me that whatever gains we make in our healing towards Wholeness is beneficial to the 10 generations of our family before us and the 10 generations after us. When I consider the hologram again, however, I realise that whatever consciousness any of us achieves, it will have a direct affect on the entire world—in fact the entire Cosmos.

So, again, in writing in your journal try not to judge your feelings about yourself or others as they arise, but express them appropriately. If you do that your relationships can be a lot healthier and you will not so readily off load them onto your loved ones. After all, why should they have to take these on board just because they love you? Journal writing alone can help you in a floundering relationship and take some of the *heat off* explosive situations, just by allowing your intense feelings some space to really let go.

Then ideally, we can, as Kahil Gibran writes on marriage:

...Love one another, but make not a bond of love:
Let it rather be a moving sea between the shores of your souls.
Fill each other's cup but drink not from one cup.
Give one another of your bread but eat not from the same loaf.
Sing and dance together and be joyous, but let each
one of you be alone,
Even as the strings of a lute are alone though they quiver with
the same music...

Expressing Your Feelings by Letter

One way of journal writing that I have personally found comforting and freeing is to write my thoughts and feelings in the form of a letter, addressed to God. (or any idea of Divinity you have). God does not wish us to carry heavy emotional loads. God wants us always to hand over our troubles.

This I gladly do, again and again. I have written countless letters in this way and handed them over to God. Usually I get a reply. The response comes in a variety of ways and can be quite exciting. The more specific my request for an answer the more clear the response I receive.

When I feel that I am in a crisis and my emotions are overwhelming me, I have experienced comfort and healing by writing a small note to God and placing this under a lighted candle. As the candle burns down I am usually aware of God's reassuring Love. I do this many times when other people who are in crisis ask me to help them. I write their names on a piece of paper with my prayer request to God, and I place this letter underneath a lighted candle. I have had numerous validations of this kind of healing through the connection to God in this way.

The Unsent Letter

Write an unsent letter to anyone you feel you want to.
This letter will never to be posted,
because it is not going to be sent.
You can freely express whatever you wish.
You can say anything you want to.
Set a time limit to write.
Light a candle to hold the Light.
If there is more to say,
write another letter the next day,
and then another
until you feel that there is no more to say…

If you want,
at the beginning of this exercise

offer the entire letter and its contents to God,
in order to

HEAL

Write a Letter to Someone Who Has Died

Sometimes we do not get to say everything we want
before someone who is important to us dies.
Sometimes it is not appropriate to say what we feel when they are alive.
Sometimes we need to finish unfinished business.
Sometimes we need to say thank you.
Sometimes we need to say I forgive you,
or
I love you.
Sometimes we need to say I love you, but I am angry at you too.
Sometimes our loved ones need to hear from us,
even when they have already left their bodies.

At the end of the letter,
give thanks to the Divine
for listening to you,
for loving you throughout,
for loving those who have passed away,
for allowing you your life.
Because without this beautiful life
you cannot grow
into
your
Wholeness.

HEAL

Intuition and Symbols

13

A word or an image is symbolic when it implies something more than its obvious and immediate meaning. It has a wider "unconscious" aspect that is never precisely defined or fully explained. Nor can one hope to define or explain it. As the mind explains the symbols it is led to ideas that lie beyond the grasp of reason.

The wheel may lead our thoughts toward the concept of a "divine" sun but at this point reason must admit its incompetence; man is unable to define a "divine" being. When, with all our intellectual limitations, we call something "divine," we have merely given it a name, which may be based on a creed but never on factual evidence.

Carl Jung—***Man and His Symbols***

From childhood we are normally trained to use the analytical mind rather than the intuitive mind. Our deeper feelings and understanding related more to our Heart and Divinity are not usually encouraged. The only outlet they may have is in certain kinds of creative artwork and religious studies. The more sensitive aspects of our Heart are pushed aside to encourage and develop our cognitive minds. Only the Divine within us can understand Divinity. The mind never will be able to go further than its boundaries of logic and three-dimensionality. Divine Truth, however, is multi-dimensional and limitless, and through symbolic thought man can make the miraculous leap between mind and soul to the depths of our Unconscious and Whole Self.

We need to be able to use our minds analytically and intelligently in order to function in society. Therefore, our personalities, the tools of our lower minds, are also encouraged to develop. The sense of *I* and its individuation is stressed as being important. Learning to take care of oneself, to look out for oneself and to make sure that one gets his/her fair share is emphasised. Competitiveness, achievement, social status and affluence are all considered necessary attributes to being a successful member of society and a good human being. The better one's rank in society, and the more one can speak with an elite dialect, the more one is accepted, honoured and served.

The qualities of the *lower mind* are, of course, useful and practical—even though their projections and understanding cannot always be trusted. If we learn well enough and are schooled correctly, we may do well in our learning, perhaps take higher studies, become successful in our work, and have high social standing. We most probably will get married, have children, and become grandparents. If we are lucky, we may live long enough to do all this in the ups and down of life and then, of course, at some point we die. What do we do then? What have we done about the finding of our eternal nature and its vast potential to realise limitless Love and Divinity?

Even though someone has had a good life and been a good person, can we say that life has been of real value if he/she dies without ever having touched True Nature? Did that life justify the amazing grace of human birth?

The less encouraged aspect of our nature is, obviously, our Divinity and its language of the Heart and Soul. In our society and whirlwind of achieving, there is no room for this. The Heart has qualities of Love that are non-competitive and selfless. The Heart is capable of surrendering and of sacrifice. It is not fooled by, and does not act in accordance with, outer man-made distinctions of class, caste, creed and affluence. The Heart has an understanding of Truth that goes beyond the limited ideas of the cerebral mind.

Many great Spiritual Masters have had little or no formal schooling, and yet their understanding goes beyond that of any eminent and learned scholars who stand before them seeking their guidance. God cannot be understood by the lower mind. God can only be known with the Higher Mind, which is related to the Heart.

At the age of 12, Jesus taught the Pharisees. In November and December 2001 I was graced to meet His Holiness the Karmapa, the

Head of the Kagyue Lineage of Tibetan Buddhism, and had the privilege to spend six weeks in His presence, both in Dharamsala and on pilgrimage to Bodhgaya. He was then a boy of 16 years of age. But, when I personally had interviews with Him or heard Him speak in public, my limited mind was unable to understand the eternal and unfathomable wisdom coming from Him. This granted a dear wish I had to know what it must have been like to sit at the feet of the boy Jesus, or in the presence of my own Guru, Sri Sathya Sai Baba, when He was a child. When I talked with the Karmapa I remembered this longing and realised that this must be a similar experience to those who had the grace to sit at the feet of other Divine Beings when they were children.

Although He attended elementary school, Sai Baba as a child had little formal education and yet He could quote profusely from the teachings of Buddha, Guru Nanak, Sri Rama Krishna, as well as the *Gita* and the *Ramanaya.* He was often heard to quote profusely from the *Vedas* and spoke eloquently in Sanskrit, a language that He never studied. Although still a child, people were dumfounded when they heard Him speak with authority on all subjects.

To ***know*** something truly and without any doubt is an attribute of the Heart. The way of knowing something truly is to ***feel*** it beyond any rational or logical method of thinking. There is a point when outer knowledge becomes irrelevant and nonessential. The learning of more facts, figures and ideas, becomes a kind of cardboard cut out in place of the real thing! The more you travel on your Spiritual Path, external information is just not enough. It is the Heart that wants to be heard and claimed and wishes to be a flowing Vehicle of Love.

The language of the Heart and the Soul is intuitive and symbolic. This is one reason why our religious traditions and churches are full of symbolic literature, rituals and images. These have their own language and wisdom that cut through the logical and rational cognitive mind. This is not to say that the lower mind does not have its place. But we must remember that its understanding is external, learned and subject to the colouring of projections, desires, and attitudes. It is always limited. The wisdom of the Heart, on the other hand, is expansive, Divine and therefore limitless. The Heart is not dualistic or conditional. It experiences everything as One.

Sri Sathya Sai Baba says:

Man has no need to seek anything outside him. He has the Universe within him in his Heart. He is potentially the Cosmic Being. He has within him the magnetic power of attraction. It is derived from the Divine.

The Heart's understanding is not schooled but intuitive. This intuitiveness goes beyond form and external comprehension. It is a direct experience of the Truth. When we can learn to control the lower mind and its attachments, its debilitating emotions and desires, it becomes purer. In this state, it then becomes a perfect accompaniment for the Heart's play. In the purifying process, discrimination is a helpful tool and one that can enable you to gain more of the wisdom of the Heart. The cultivation of peace of mind and devotion are also a powerful duo.

Symptoms, Causes and Effects

As we **HEAL** towards Wholeness there is a point when the Heart Chakra begins to be activated and purified. The lower mind serves the Root, Sacral and Solar Plexus Chakras. These are related to the external self in the external and material world. When a person's evolving is ready, more activation in awareness begins in relation to the Heart Chakra, and Its qualities of compassion, selflessness, purity and devotion begin to arise.

This is the beginning of the end of the enthronement of the lower mind's dualistic and judgmental projections and disunity. As the Heart Chakra opens more and more, clear feelings of Divine Love will be felt, and with this an understanding of its Truth. This awareness will in time help to purify the mind, and its discriminatory powers will become purer also. Both of these gifts, pure discrimination and the awareness of Divine Love will lead you to Wholeness.

As our beings continue to purify, the Throat Chakra is activated with an increase of the purity, power and truth of communication on all levels. Our expression often increases and we become more creative. Dreams, symbols, imagery, and singing, hearing and writing can all be enhanced.

Good or true communication is not merely being able to interact or transmit ideas, feelings and thoughts with others. It is also about being able to interact with different levels/bodies of oneself, of the unconscious and subconscious aspects of ourselves. Some people call this *being in touch with yourself.*

When the Throat Chakra begins to activate, there is usually an initial outpouring of psychic waves of subconscious and unconscious material in the form of dreams, awakening of senses, visions, inner voices and so on. The floodgates of expression that were blocked are suddenly released, and waves of energy are running through you. They carry much material from the past and from the depths of the unconscious. Most of the feelings you will suddenly experience are very temporary and are merely movements dancing with the waves. In the blue lake of the throat, peace can be found like the sound of the waves of inner silence.

As the Ajna Centre (Third Eye) purifies, our intuition, inner vision and outer vision as well as will and perception increases. Our seeing changes, and we observe more Truth—That which is beyond duality and Maya.

There is another seeing which resides in the Ajna Centre. This seeing is pure and clear and not distorted by our personalities or biases. It can be referred to as clairvoyance, but this inner vision can also be known as Intuition. This does not necessarily mean that you will see images externally with your *clairvoyant eye.* The vision may be purely internal—an understanding even. However, when one receives such a vision one has no doubt that it has come from a purer source than the lower mind and its senses and that it is Truth.

With these visions, I have discovered the qualities of purity and detachment along with luminosity about them. You cannot forget them. Ordinary projected thoughts will leave you within a very short time but the lucidity of the imagery, which comes from your inner eye of Truth, will remain with you for years.

When our Awakening Energy (sometimes referred to as Kundalini), moves to the Sahasrara, the Crown Chakra, our Spirituality, Divinity, Knowing (rather than thinking), Equanimity, Bliss and Self Realisation are activated.

Certain symptoms can be felt during the purification of these centres. Often, someone going through this purification finds that his or her rational mind can get a bit muddled or confused. People find that they are forgetful or cannot remember certain details while simultaneously having vivid and symbolic visions. This is a very frightening thing to experience, especially if one has had a strong reliance on the lower mind faculties. Spiritual excersises like meditation can help you to find more *internal space,* but the reasoning mind is not particularly at home with emptiness.

Some experience these awakenings as though the ground beneath them is shifting or, in fact, has disappeared. For a while, they may feel as if out on a limb. It is understandable, as what they considered to be known valid facts are not reliable anymore. Sometimes there can be confusion as to what is truth and what can be relied upon at all. As was written earlier, the cognitive mind will not be so in control and this can be upsetting. The confusion is the result of a new *balancing of the language of the mind and the language of the Heart*

At this time also the outer lives of people can transform, for as the old values, say, of worldly acquisition and success are replaced by new ones of, say, sacrifice and devotion, they no longer correspond to the older ways of living. These new values require space and time to unfold, and we need the necessary space and time to explore them.

God and God's timing, however, are perfect and one can witness, again and again, how someone's life will change accordingly and synchronistically to incorporate the increasing new integration of the Heart's values.

Bliss and depression may not seem related, but they are two sides of the same coin. There are certain spiritual stages some people go through where they will seesaw from bliss to depression until such time that equanimity takes over—in such a place of equal-mindedness *one can be in the world but not of it.* Here, the constant thrashing or bouncing from bliss to depression ceases. You may also seesaw in your other perceptions, emotions and feelings as well as your intuition and awareness. Personal experiences differ with every individual. These will have a great bearing on the spiritual experiences one has had this lifetime, and how one reacts to them and the idea of one's growing spirituality.

I have observed what I came to define as *spiritual schizophrenia* sometimes in people on the spiritual path. In severe situations this might be mistaken as a psychotic disturbance. It involves a mental cutting off from the idea of one's Spiritual Self, repulsion even, and a deep engagement in the material world followed by the opposite and other end of the extreme. When the seesaw contains the extreme dualities of, say, besotted love and total rejection a balance is produced. Thus, the individual can become stuck in the apparent schizophrenia for some time, until something comes to shift the balance.

Intuitive Knowing and Symbols

As we become more attuned with the Heart and Soul Wisdom, we will *know more.* This is a knowing which goes beyond any that external education can give us, no matter how good. This sense of knowing is instant and needs no reasoning. It needs no working out. One just knows. This is not to be confused with the projections of the mind that are filled with impure thoughts and emotions like jealousy, resentment and selfishness—which are often biased, accusatory and judgmental in relation to others and ourselves.

Symbolic language can arise at any stage in our evolving. As we have seen, a symbol is a multidimensional energy. It is also multifaceted. Therefore, in one symbol you may perceive many levels of meaning and experience depths of understanding. The meaning required by you will be realised by you. Only you can have the true understanding because it is your symbol and it has arisen from your personal awareness or from the Collective Unconscious especially for you.

For example, if you suddenly begin to see crucifixes everywhere you go, and you have never noticed them before and they appear also in your dreams, your personal relationship to a crucifix will have a direct bearing on the meaning of this symbolic message for you. You may have to contemplate on it or you may not need to. You might have a spontaneous recognition of all levels of this symbol's meaning.

The Heart and Soul's Divine language reflects Infinity. I have found, for example, that whatever my Guru, Sri Sathya Sai Baba says is *highly Symbolic, even though He may be using simple and seemingly banal remarks.* After a period of time and in retrospect, however, I experience His words as having multidimensional meaning and they have answered many questions on many levels.

Although there can be a basic uniformity and understanding of symbols and what they represent, the particular understanding of them is unique to you. Symbols cannot really be understood in fullness by looking at reference books and reading other people's interpretations of them. These reference books are good for seeing how Archetypal symbols are generally understood by people throughout the world, regardless of differences in language and origin. However, although there is sameness, each symbol's very unique message has to be individually and personally interpreted.

We each have what the Tibetan Buddhists call *Karmic Vision.* How we see something, anything and interpret it, depends on our complete history and experience. This means the experience and subsequent perception from all our lives, and in all forms. The symbol of water, for instance, may be cooling and pleasurable for one person but for another it may mean drowning.

One only needs to look at the Archetypal symbol of *God* to see how this can differ in representation and understanding with different people. For example, God is a personal friend to one person and to others God might be Cosmic Consciousness or Right Action. Yet, to still others God might be hateful. No one else can have the same relationship to God as you. Your relationship with Divinity is as unique as your entire history of perception and understanding is unique. Therefore, no one can understand and interpret God for you. Have you ever noticed how you have felt when someone has tried to impose his or her idea of God on you? It is the same with all symbolic images; most of us do not like to be told how to interpret them.

Symbols are also healing agents in that they have a multidimensional healing effect as well as a perceptual impact. If, in the course of any healing, you experience the arising of a symbolic image, remember that it will inherently have its own unique way of helping you to HEAL you. I have found that Sai Baba's personal words have healed me in this way.

Even if you do not understand what the symbol means, it can be sufficient to just contemplate on it. The very contemplating on the symbol will allow its multidimensional healing to do its work. Symbols are also understood more than words by your Unconscious and subconscious minds. They are indeed more powerful than the mere expressions of your normal and everyday way of using words. However, words—if treated with respect and spoken with spiritual intent—are also very powerful.

In the beginning was the Word.

OM is the primordial sound considered to be the sound of Creation. Sound generates movement. In this way the sound caused by Creation gave rise to Its movement throughout the Cosmos. All the different sounds we make are, therefore, variations on the theme of OM. When you speak with intent and respect you are in touch with this power of creation. It is in this way too that Mantras are endowed with spiritual and healing energy. Using words in such a way is symbolic and ritualistic. The words are potent and soaked in Divinity.

Can I Trust This or Not?

Particularly in the early stages of the Higher Self's awakening, many people flounder with regard to understanding whether they are receiving intuitive Wisdom, or whether it is something from their lower minds. The mind will not want to step down from its elevated platform, of course, and it will try to find ways of tricking you. The Heart and Soul never lie. So, how do you know if you are receiving guidance/Wisdom from your Heart or from your mind?

Sai Baba says:

It is this heart that reaches the goal. Follow the heart, for a pure heart seeks beyond the intellect—it gets inspired.

It has been my experience that when the Heart and Soul speak there is a heightened awareness, detachment and luminosity. If I have an outer or internal symbolic vision the message is more lucid, vivid and direct, than any I might receive from the mind. The impact of the Divine message does not fade with time either. The thoughts of the mind can fade quite quickly, but the image and quality of divinely inspired symbols remain.

This makes sense when you realise that the Divine symbol is one that speaks to all levels of your being and not just to your consciously aware mind. It speaks to the different levels of your astral and mental bodies, and recites the words of your Soul. As your understanding of the symbol is integrated, your conscious mind will increasingly have more understanding also. This integration will have its own perfect timing.

Another way to verify whether you are receiving a symbol from your mind or Heart is to ask your *Conscience*. Your Conscience is a Divine quality and is one of the attributes of your Spiritual Heart. Your Conscience is not self-seeking and is Goodness.

The River of Life, Death and Rebirth

Before I came to India, I thought I had a comfortable life, and had decided that I was on the correct path. I did not envisage that it would change. I was working in private practice as a psychotherapist, healer, intuitive, Dream Group leader and teacher. My life appeared full. I worked from 9 a.m. in the morning until 9 p.m. at night most days. There was little time left to think, let alone make any further decisions. Yet, I was aware of a kind of nudging that there was something else, but I did not know what.

I received a phone call one day from a friend to tell me that a very special teacher from the Himalayas was travelling from India for the first time, a Rinpoche, and my friend asked if I would I like to meet him. The following day was mentioned. I looked at my diary, which, as I knew it would be, was full and I said that I would not be able to make it. Perhaps another time I said. I was told that this would probably be impossible as the Rinpoche would immediately travel to Ireland then back to India. I have to confess that this did not bother me too much. I was so busy and my life had become such a routine that I was in any case reluctant to change my plans or go out of my way for anything else.

The next day I did not give the possible meeting any further thought. I was too occupied! I finished work, quite exhausted at around 8 p.m. and I lied down. Immediately, I saw the vision of a large screen that opened up in front of me. It was around three feet in front of me. On this screen, I saw myself standing at the edge of a fast-flowing river. Although I could see myself, as if in a movie, my consciousness was also present in the "I" standing by the river's edge.

I was the seer and the one who was experiencing at the same time. As I looked into the fast-moving river below me, images of men, women and children within the water, rushed past me, as though trying to get my attention. But, before I could connect with any of them, the water quickly carried them downstream. The river was full of people and its fullness seemed limitless. I was aware on a multidimensional level that they had all lived and died, that some had difficult deaths and some more easy. But, they looked tormented to me and the whole scene was quite terrifying.

As I looked deep into this stream of what I could describe as a mass of fast-flowing Consciousness, I felt a Divine Presence standing to my right side, just behind me. It was as though my mind became still and everything became silent. This Divine Presence leaned closer and said in my ear, "Take a good look, because you are next."

As I heard the words I realised without any doubt what this Presence meant. I was going to die. I was going to fall into this river of Consciousness and I, as I knew myself, would be no more. These people I could see were all me! They were all the lives I had gone through and they were all the deaths I had experienced. It had gone on for aeons. The question was—Did I want to die again as I am now, or die free? I was shaken. I felt quite frightened. The scene had greatly disturbed me. Yet, I knew that it was the Truth.

The next day, I received another phone call from my friend. I was told how Rinpoche had begun speaking around 8 p.m. and how he gave a talk on life and death. He also spoke about how we should be aware that we are all going to die one day and that until we are free we will remain in Samsara. He gave the analogy that all our births and deaths can be seen as a flowing river…

I realised that as Rinpoche spoke, although I was not physically present and had never met him, I directly experienced the talk in a highly symbolic and evocative way. I felt acutely sad that I had not taken the opportunity to meet him and especially as I had connected so strongly with his teachings. I realised my arrogance and foolishness. How could I have not made the space for the opportunity for this Truth?

About two weeks later, I received another call saying that Rinpoche had unexpectedly come back for a few days. I was given a second chance! I cancelled my appointments and I confirmed the time that I could come the next day. At that time I had never met a Rinpoche and knew very little about Tibetan Buddhist teachings. When I met him, as soon as I sat down, I felt disconcerted as tears flowed and flowed. I could not stop them.

He asked me about my profession and was very interested in the Dreamwork I did. He told me a dream he had of his Guru who had died. He asked me to interpret the dream. At the time of the dream

Rinpoche's Guru was still alive. I instantly saw how Rinpoche's Guru had shown his coming death, through the highly symbolic imagery which Rinpoche described seeing in his dream. This dream and Rinpoche's sharing of it was my first teaching from him. I learned about the connection that goes beyond death between the Guru and disciple.

Understandably, the course of my life changed and within six months it had turned upside down. I found myself staying in Sikkim with Rinpoche and his family, undergoing intense training with this Master.

The message of the symbol and the imagery in the river vision affected me and transformed me more than if any doctor had told me that I was going to die the next day. Also, the synchronicity of the vision and Rinpoche's speech could not be ignored. Not only that, but the message from beyond the limitations of time and space actually reached into my concretised world and spoke to me.

Messages for Others

When you must give someone intuitive advice, be cautious. Be aware that you must be free from any investment in being right or wrong. Prayer and surrender are necessary before you begin. Through your unconscious mind's projections, you can have ideas about what is good for someone or not. You can also have ideas about them personally. Only God knows us. We cannot possibly begin to understand the *Wholeness* of someone, and we need to continually remind ourselves of this before giving out messages of what we think they need or not. Also, our egos always have desires of power seeking and control. Not only that, but we can project our own fears and desires in this way and pass them onto others in the wrapping of a so-called vision or symbol.

This, of course, is one of the pitfalls for people who work in the psychic realm. When your Heart is still impure and held in the powerful grip of the lower mind you are likely to say something completely inappropriate and perhaps damaging to another in the name of psychic seeing, hearing and sensing.

I taught Psychic Development in the Edinburgh College of Parapsychology for over seven years. During that time, I was able to explore these kinds of pitfalls as well as the advantages of psychic awareness for others' benefit. If you are in doubt, one way to bypass your own possible prejudices and projections is to use symbols and to pass on the symbol for the person concerned to interpret him/herself. When you are in doubt, say nothing. If you feel strongly impressed to say something then first connect with your Conscience, pray for guidance, surrender your ego as much as you can and all possible outcomes *for the good of all concerned.*

Ask Yourself

Is what I have to say uplifting and helpful?
Will it possibly frighten or hurt someone?
Is there anything in the saying of this for me?
What is likely to happen if I say nothing?
Am I sure what my motive is?
Is it an act of Compassion and Divine Love?
Or, will it make me feel powerful?

HEAL

Remember that whatever you say can have a lasting effect on someone, consciously, unconsciously and subconsciously. It is your responsibility to be very clear as to why you are saying something and what your particular reasons are. You need to reflect on this frequently and this intense examination of your actions and desires will help you to connect with your Heart more and more. The more you connect with the Divine Love in your Heart the more you will be Whole and will be of true help to others. Always try to offer the fruits of all your actions to God. Surrender yourself and whatever you are saying to Divinity and you will see how miraculously and unexpectedly you will be used.

Things Are Never What They Seem

One day a man who was very depressed came to me for some spiritual and psychic guidance. He told me that he had been depressed for some time. He felt so hopeless that he wanted me to psychically see if there was going to be any happiness for him.

I agreed to do this and when I connected psychically, I felt tremendous happiness coming for him. I did not know how this was going to be, but I felt that everything was going to be all right for him and would work out and that he was going to enter one of the happiest times of his life. All I could see was tremendous brightness and light. I felt that this happiness would continue until he died, and I told him so.

There were no logical reasons to support what I felt. His story was so sad and his depression so severe, but I gave him purely what I was feeling and seeing. I did not try to understand it because I could not. He left, however, feeling quite uplifted and I did not see him again.

About a year later a woman made an appointment to see me. When we met she asked me if I remembered the man who had come to me, who had been very depressed and whom I had told was going to be very happy. I did remember and said, yes. She told me that she was the man's wife but that he had died a short time ago. She also told me that after his session with me he had become increasingly happier, and as a result his life had become happier too. Then unexpectedly he died. What was so remarkable was that this had been the happiest time of his life and he had died happy. HEAL

I realised that I had been used to enable this man to be happy before he died. In the chapter on Death you may remember that how we feel when we die is the predisposition of our next birth, or the way in which we journey in the afterlife. I was grateful that he had died happy. I was also aware that I had been given absolutely no indication that he would die so soon—only that he was going to be very happy. We can never know the full picture. At such times, I trust that I am a mere instrument. We can only know what God wishes us to know. And only God knows when we will die. But, here, God wanted this man, who had been sad for most of his life, to die happy and this is just what he did.

Symbol Synchronicity

Synchronicity, or meaningful coincidence, assumes that nothing is random, or by chance. It assumes that everything and everyone affects everything else. Because of this, possible future outcomes can be divined or measured, and our hidden actions, as well as those more conscious, can be examined and met with more awareness.

The future is a combination of the result of the past and present. But time is multifaceted and multidimensional and synchronicity reflects this phenomenon. In my experience, although much is pre-ordained and is our destiny, nothing is unchangeable. God can change anything God wishes to. The future is an effect of your present actions and choices, and the degree of consciousness of these actions is also dependent on your past actions and choices as well.

Whatever you make conscious and are able to integrate will have an effect on the happening and timing of events and your relationship to them. People who begin to connect with their spiritual energies have evidence of these phenomena. They notice that not only does everything become more meaningful and emotionally and psychically heightened in a significantly profound way, but that synchronistic happenings occur more frequently and strongly as their consciousness increases.

Everything and everyone is a mirror to us, in this, our relative reality. The more conscious you become, the more the world will clearly reflect to you, your state of mind, consciousness and being. Most notably, Shamans have used this method of awareness of their external environment as a mirror, in order to make sense of their environment in relationship to them and to divine future potentials for themselves and others.

For example, some North American Indians see a bat as a symbol of death/rebirth. If someone undergoing a crisis is contemplating on events happening in their life and there is the appearance of a bat, they will know that The Source, Divine Wisdom, through the reflection of Nature, is confirming to them that what they are going through is a death/rebirth.

During the spiritual retreats I lead, there is usually space given for people to commune with nature and to use this time as a *Vision Quest.* In this contemplation and witnessing, they note everything they encounter and experience as part of The Source's reflecting Wisdom, revealing their current consciousness, obstacles and potential. In these highly meditative and contained settings, many seeming miraculous insights and happenings can take place for the participants. But if we are aware enough, they can happen anywhere and at any time. The following is an account of Divine synchronistic mirroring in my own home:

There Is No Safe Place—Only Truth

Following my meeting with Rinpoche and the river vision, as well as a powerful and unexpected meeting with the Dalai Lama, just before this, I was increasingly aware of an inner urgency that I needed to go deeper in my search for the Self. But, in order to do this I was aware that I would need to change the entire pattern of my life. I had vivid dreams at that time also, which indicated I should travel and meet with teachers who could help me in this search. But, as usual, my ego self was resistant. My life was quite comfortable, it argued. I had family near me, a good home, was successful in my work, had good friends and was very popular and busy. I was doing good and useful work so why should I relinquish all this in search of an urge, my ego continued to tell me.

Although my conceptions had been inwardly shattered by the river vision, and I could not forget it, my ego reasoning at that time was that if my life was flowing so smoothly, why should I make any unnecessary disruptions for myself and my patients, clients and groups. Also, deep down, I was afraid and I felt safe and secure staying at home and in familiar and comfortable surroundings.

I made an internal decision to do nothing and to stay where I was. The thought of leaving my comfortable home, income and fulfilling work was too disturbing. Of course, at that time, I went unconscious on the fact that what is planned for us is not really up to us but up to God !

Not long after the decision to stay home, I was lying safely and comfortably in my bed one morning. I got up to get ready for the day's work. When I was in the kitchen I heard an explosion coming from my bedroom. There was a tremendous bang. I ran into the bedroom to see that the ceiling had come down on my bed. There was a man's legs dangling through it from the above flat. There was rubble, stones and dirt everywhere, but most of it lying on my bed, from where I had not long moved.

My neighbours from the flat above had been doing some repair work to the floor, had removed the floorboards and the man had slipped, fell and had gone straight through the remaining partition and become stuck in my ceiling !

No one was hurt. I was insured, and so, within a short time, the ceiling was repaired and painted and everything was as though back to normal. But I could not return to normal—now I did not feel so safe and secure in my comfortable bedroom, bed and life.

Even though this event happened, I still felt resistant to change. However, the shock was enough to make me tentatively think about taking a year's sabbatical in order to study meditation and have the space to go deeper in my spiritual search. I looked into costs for the possible journey and it amounted to around £3000.

But, after some further consideration, which no doubt still had the foundation of fear of change as its base, I decided again that there was no need for me to go anywhere. I was doing good work, I argued and it was better I stay where I was.

Shortly after I made the second decision to remain with things as they were, angry and distressed neighbours who lived in the basement beneath my flat contacted me urgently. Their ceiling had fallen in, and they told me that it was due to water leaking from my kitchen—most probably from my washing machine. An engineer was called in, but he could not find anything wrong with the washing machine or where there was water leakage from anywhere in my house. However, he said that there was no doubt that the water had been slowly leaking from my water pipes and that there was evidence for the leak but no evidence for the source. He was baffled. This was even more disconcerting, because whatever the cause, it could not be externally seen or fixed. My conviction to stay in my comfortable life, which was now becoming quite uncomfortable, was so strong that I was blinded to what was really being shown to me by these two synchronistic events.

My insurance company would not pay for the repair of the damage this time, as they said that it was my fault and that I should have repaired the washing machine. I argued that the engineer had found nothing wrong with the washing machine. And they argued that the water was coming from somewhere in my flat and so it was my fault. I felt under this constant threat of water leakage that no one could find the cause of, and that if this continued I might end up bankrupt.

I tried to get the insurance company broker to change his mind. In the meantime, I received a bill from my neighbours in the basement for the repair of their ceiling, which amounted to £3000.

When I saw the sum involved, everything "fell into place," and I was immediately aware of the synchronicity of these symbolic outer happenings. I saw the reality and the Maya fell away. I realised that God was showing me that there is no secure or safe place. Not only had my ceiling caved in above my bed—my world symbolically fallen in on me, but the ground beneath me had also fallen away. I had no safe and secure place left on which to stand. And the money I should have used to go on my sabbatical was now to be paid as a penalty! Because of my resistance, I had not wanted to see the Truth, but the reflections of the Truth, ruthlessly and relentlessly came until I had no choice but to do so.

Shortly after this realisation, as if to confirm my understanding, I had a dream where I was standing on the corner of a street in Edinburgh. Grey tenement buildings surrounded me. It was misty and damp and the sky was grey. Everything was grey and felt grey. Yet, I was radiant and I was wearing a colourful summer dress. But, there was no door open to me into any of the buildings. There was no one else to be seen. There was no where for me.

After I awoke that morning, I went to the travel agents to organise my leaving for a year. I did not know it then, but until this time, nine years later, I would not return to my beloved Edinburgh to stay, and my life, as I knew it, was never to be the same again. All I knew was that I had to go. I did not know why or what would happen and everything felt uncertain. But I knew that the only sure, secure and certain thing I could trust was the Truth. I had to follow this wherever it led me and trust Divine Wisdom. My initial destination was Sikkim to be with Rinpoche to receive further teachings and transmissions from him.

Within a few days of making the commitment to go, and booking my flights, I received a telephone call from the insurance company to tell me that they had decided to give me the money for the repairs. Yes, it was £3000, the exact amount I needed to make my initial journey.

Divinity affirmed to me Its approval!

Prayer and Meditation In Our Healing Towards Wholeness

14

God exists, but is invisible. He rotates the sun and the moon to drive out the darkness from the universe. He props up millions of stars high up in the sky, preventing them from tumbling down. He whirls the world round, without an axle to the wheel. He spreads the invisible winds and controls the ocean from engulfing the lands. He holds aloft the canopy of the skies overhead without its crashing down. He works unseen behind the scenes making the world dance on the screen. God does exist.

Sri Sathya Sai Baba

We cannot fully **HEAL** without encompassing the idea of God. This idea need not be the acceptance of a form of God. Many experience *God* as Love or Truth. But, the point is that we have to believe in something vaster or greater than our ego-selves in order to **HEAL**. Otherwise, our capacity to **HEAL** is constantly limited by the smallness of our egos and their controlling thoughts and delusions.

If you do not like the term, *God,* or even feel offended or antagonistic to It as some people I have met, think about what you do believe in that is greater, wiser and vaster than you and which you can look up to. Do you believe in, for example, Truth, Love, Wisdom, Innate Intelligence or Wholeness?

Whatever you believe in that you feel you can aspire to, which you feel is greater than you is more than sufficient to pray to. It is That which is your Inspirer, your Illuminator and your Guru, your God, as you journey towards Wholeness.

Sai Baba has said that only God can **HEAL**. Although I can be called a *healer,* and I have sometimes had spectacular results, I know with an absolute certainty that Sai Baba is right and that only God can **HEAL**. I am sure there are many people around who can help themselves and others to HEAL but they are merely *instruments* of God. Whatever healing happens is a result of God, of Divinity permeating through the *healing* and Its Will—not the healer's will. We can confirm this by the evidence of the many times when healing, as we wish for it, does not happen. This occurs because God did not will the healing to take place as we had hoped. God, in this instance, had other plans.

So, importantly, we first need to surrender the concept that we are the *doers* either in our own or others' healing, and surrender ourselves to a greater power than us, be it called God, Jesus, Allah, Buddha, Love, Truth, Light, Divinity or whatever.

How can we, who are operating through our ego-minds and their ignorance, fully know what is required and when? There are times when we will be Divinely inspired, when we sense without any doubt a *rightness* in our knowing, but until we are completely Whole, we are not operating from that Divine Wisdom at all times. What we will be doing is functioning from a mind that has dualistic notions, which has judgements and preferences, and which therefore has tainted vision. Only God knows the Divine Total View of Absolute Wisdom of the past, present and future, of all aspects of a situation and what is perfect for all those concerned.

You can surrender yourself to Divinity, through prayer. Prayer can take a multitude of forms and can be as personally unique as you are. It might even be that your form of prayer is simply an understanding that what you are doing is automatically handed over to God. It might be in the form of a small ritual, kneeling down or placing your hands together in supplication and saying something like:

I offer this healing and myself
to the Wisdom and Compassion
of Divine Will and Love.
Let it be Thy Will and not my will
for the good of all concerned.

A surrendering affirmation is a prayer. It is to your idea of God. In particular, it is a healthy reminder to you to, *get out of the way,* so that the true Grace of healing can flow through you.

When you do any practical type of healing, like the Dream Work or Journal Work outlined in the previous chapters, you can include a small simple prayer or affirmation at the beginning and at the end of your session. A closing prayer can be something like:

Thank You, Dear God,
for being with me in every step I take
and for allowing me the time and the strength
to witness the miracle of Your Healing Love.

Thank You, Dear God,
for being with me at this time.
In gratitude,
I surrender to Your Will Divine.

But you can also begin the day with a surrendering prayer and offer your coming experiences, your happiness and trials and even your sadness over to God as a means of your healing towards Wholeness. In this way, you live your daily life with the awareness that God is healing you towards Wholeness through every moment, and every happening.

Ritual is a containing and fundamentally powerful act. It reassures all levels of your psyche that it is being held. Your psyche feels protected and contained, and it facilitates an understanding and integration of what you are feeling on every level of your being. Ritual can cut right through the conscious mind like a sword, and enter the unconscious and subconscious minds and create the conditions for deep healing to take place. Spiritually, it can also help you to make the Divine leap from your lower mind to your higher mind and connect with your Divinity.

Sai Baba says:

Every RITUAL has a SPIRITUAL significance behind it. When compared to the first word "Ritual" the second word contains three extra letters S.P.I. It means every ritual can impart S.P.I. i.e., Spiritual Power (to the) Individual who performs the ritual, only if Special attention is Paid (to the) Inner meaning and significance of the ritual.

Our psyches can be like little children. They can easily feel overwhelmed, or insecure, like a little child does, when he or she suddenly realises his/her parent is nowhere to be seen. All at once, the world feels too big. When you are about to transform, to change, to take off those *old raincoats,* you need to feel sure and secure. You also need to feel safe enough to even hand yourself over to the Love of God. This is how ritual can help you. Psychically, I feel that ritual is like God, (our parents) lifting us (small little children) from a busy dangerous traffic-filled street, to the safety of a secure little playpen or garden.

Likewise, as we are multidimensional beings and much of our unconscious and subconscious is not available to us directly or easily, ritual connects our awareness to these levels. Performing a ritual is accepted and understood by our subconscious in a way our normal thoughts, actions or words cannot be. As you read earlier in the chapter on Symbols and Intuition, your subconscious mind is at home with symbols or symbolic actions in a way the lower mind is not. Ritual includes evocative symbolic action and not just thought. Your ritual, even though simple, like lighting a candle, will, if done with sincerity and honouring, instantaneously connect you to all levels of your being and your Divinity.

Some people like to ritualise the time that they pray and the place that they formally pray in. Your ritual spot can be a little corner of your room or a small room or even a cupboard that is large enough for you to sit in. I have often used small, enclosed spaces like this to pray in. And, of course, there is the ritual of going to a church or temple and being part of the spiritual practices there.

When I was working daily in my private psychotherapy and healing practice in Edinburgh, I would ritually wash my hands and light some incense to honour the beginning and completion of each session, and to formally create a psychic boundary between each patient. This small conscious action, immediately provided a powerful conscious and unconscious way of detaching, which enabled me to be fully with each one in the individual and personal way that each of them deserved and needed.

Prayer as an Offering of Love to Love

The whole creation was designed as a test for man. By our conduct in this world we disclose whether we want the Lord or His gifts. God will not tell you that you should desire Him above all else, because He wants your love to be freely given, without "prompting." That is the whole secret in the game of this universe. He who created us yearns for our love. He wants us to give it spontaneously without His asking. Our love is the only thing God does not possess, unless we choose to bestow it. So, you see, even the Lord has something to attain: our love. And we shall never be happy until we give it.

Paramahansa Yogananda—***How You Can Talk with God***

What is prayer? It is offering yourself, your love to Divine Love. When you do this fully and completely, with no conditions, no desires, no expectations that your love will even be returned, you will be Whole. When you surrender your love to Divinity, your love will remember its Truth and become Divine.

Sai Baba says about Divine Love:

The Shruthi (Vedha) declares "It did not originate from the firmament. It did not grow from the earth. It has no birth and death. It is all pervading. It emerges from the heart when the knots of ignorance are broken."

Prayer is not a request to be used just in times of need. We actually *need* God all the time. But usually we do not even think of prayer until we feel that we need, or we are in crisis and we have nowhere else to turn to. God is not usually the first option we turn to, but generally the last. It is the same with love. Often we are prepared to give our love away to anything or anyone that superficially appeals to us, or is attractive to us, yet the last thing we normally consider is to give our love to God, to That, to which we owe everything we have.

In our love for God we can, with awareness, pray in supplication to the Divine and offer ourselves in love, requesting that we be continual vehicles of God's Love and Grace for the healing of ourselves and others towards Wholeness.

Any kind of healing practice can be a form of prayer. Whether it is writing in a journal, speaking with a client in a therapy session, or a self-healing session. In this way we honour the sacredness of these opportunities to **HEAL.** *In this way also, we can be more connected to God and receive the Grace of God more easily.*

Healing can never be a technique. It is the movement of Compassionate Love towards Unity and Divine Wholeness. Expressing love in this way unconditionally and selflessly is an *action of healing* directly from the Heart, and is an expression of the Heart's language of Love.

The formality or the technique, the vehicle or means, is like the ritual, and helps us to focus. It is our intent that matters. This immediately allows Divine Energy to flow in any action or thought. *Your intent is your prayer* and it cuts through any obstacle, time and space. This is how absent healing works. Absent healing is nothing less than a prayer. We can say a prayer for anyone in the world, and if we say this with intent, it will be received through the Divine Messenger of Love.

Even if a *healer* does not believe in Divinity, if he or she sincerely wishes to help and feels compassion for a person/situation or his/her self this is enough for Divine Love to flow, and so the healing works!

Meditation and Healing Towards Wholeness

Meditation is your oneness with God, your potential Wholeness with God. The practice of the technique allows you to be able to connect with God. Meditation helps you to do this by enabling you to practice how to ignore your thoughts. Meditation is not necessarily about sitting still for hours in the lotus position (unless you really want to do this and find this fulfilling). Whatever way you remember in a concentrated and focussed way that you are one with the Divine, with God, is meditation.

You can experience this contemplation, when giving or receiving healing to self or to others. For example, when I place my hands on someone *to give them hands-on-healing* I usually visualise sacred symbols or internally chant mantras. Each time I move my hands I repeat the chant and visualisation or both, again and again, until the session is complete. In this way, the healing session becomes a meditation.

I also ask my patients to allow their minds to rest in the location of their Heart Chakra as much as possible and if their thoughts arise as they do, to try not to follow them. Eventually, I tell them, these thoughts may rest also for a while. In this way, the patient experiences a deep meditation during the healing session.

Those of you who have been initiated into Reiki II healing can meditate on the Reiki symbols with each hand move. This is how I teach people to use their second-degree level Reiki symbols and their Master Reiki symbol. One can visualise the symbols on the area of the body in question and internally chant the name of the symbol. In Reiki there are normally four symbols (including the Master symbol), and I use all four with each hand move. The result is an extremely meditative experience, which benefits both the healer and the one receiving the healing.

But you do not have to be initiated into Reiki in order to do this. To concentrate on the word HEAL, for example, and visualise what this symbolically means to you can be just as powerful. You can improvise as you wish. The important point is that you connect in whichever way is most sacred and honouring to you.

You can do this with any hands-on-healing techniques, such as spiritual healing, aromatherapy, reflexology, massage, shiatsu, cranial-sacral therapy and so on.

In placing your hands on yourself or another in an act of healing you can also think of your image of the Divine, standing behind you, to the front of you and on each side of you, above and below you. You can then visualise this Divine Power being transmitted from your hands to you (self-healing), or to another.

Many people think of pure white Light when they give healing. They visualise themselves as pure Light, transmitting pure Light to the receiver. In helping to keep one's thoughts still, any Divinely felt image could be used in this way. Retaining the image and thought of Divinity throughout the healing is a meditation. Christians may visualise the form of Jesus or the Sacred Heart. Buddhists may visualise the Buddha or perhaps you may wish to visualise a sacred symbol like the OM or Cross.

Remember that healing is:

Meditation in Action.

To begin,
pray and surrender yourself to the Divine in Love to Love.
Then,
do the healing meditation.
Then,
give thanks in a prayer of gratitude.

HEAL

The thank you is in anticipation of the outcome and is a heartfelt affirming that your prayers have been answered. There is no doubt that they will be answered according to:

Thy will and not my will.

There is no point in praying as a kind of polite lip service. If you truly believe that your prayer is being heard and will be answered, then the *thank you* is a natural burst of gratefulness from your heart and not just a polite ending!

In an exercise like Journal Work or Dream Work, you can again focus on That in you which is Divine.

Firstly

Pray and offer your love to the Divine.
Surrender all your concepts of what the answer may be.
Visualise God,
above you, below you, behind you, before you, and to each side of you.
Ask God to be with you as you "work,"
and to help you find the Truth.
When you finish,
offer a prayer of gratitude
for the Divine help and Presence you have been given.

HEAL

This simple and easy ritualised way of working will help you to get your ego out of the way and allow Divine Inspiration to flow through you. You will, I am sure, feel God close to you, provoking you and helping you.

Sathya Sai Baba says,

Through meditation, you have to develop the sense of oneness with the Divine. The practice of meditation leads to proximity to the Lord. The first stage in the process is continuous contemplation of the Divine. Think about the Lord in whatever action you do. Then you achieve nearness to God.

Meditation is about being near to God. In healing towards Wholeness you are praying that in this nearness God will use you as an instrument of Divine Will. This way of being with God does not need to end when a certain session or period of time is over. Why then push God away when some task has been done? Try to stay with the closeness by remembering God as much as is possible in whatever you do, for the rest of your day—day after day. Offer all that you do to the Divine as a gift, and your life can have a whole new meaning in healing towards Wholeness.

I know that God's power is limitless; and as I am made in His image, I too, have the strength to overcome all obstacles.

Paramahansa Yogananda—*Scientific Healing Affirmations*

Self-Healing

15

What a strange vision I am enjoying.
God (Rama) is in me and I am in God.
It is a wondrous manifestation,
Bereft of all form.
God is in me and I am in God.
I am an album of beautiful pictures of love;
All its secrets and sacrifices exist in me,
I am in love with my own beauty,
For God is in me and I am in God.

Songs of Enlightenment—Poems of Swami Rama Tirtha

Before I began to receive glimpses of Divine Love I might not have understood Sri Swami Rama Tirtha's words. However, *one morning I actually awakened to discover that I had fallen in love with myself.* This came as a result of intensive self-healing.

I was flabbergasted. This was a new awareness for me, and I had never felt anything like it before. It followed an intense time of self-searching, healing, intensive Dreamwork, emotional release and Journal Work. I had not realised, before having this feeling, how much I had not loved myself or how much I was in need of the healing. The love had absolutely nothing to do with the way I looked, or anything I had done. It was completely unconditional, spontaneous and it was just wonderful. This love accepted me and thought I was the most wonderful being in the world.

This experience was, I feel, a huge breakthrough in my journey towards Wholeness. I knew that I needed healing and I was driven to find ways of achieving this, but I had no idea that this would be one of the results. To begin with, I felt like a teenager who had become infatuated. I was consumed with this love and the intensity lasted for a few months. But later I began to realise that this love I felt was the emerging of the healing force of Divine Love within me, loving *me*. And this was the beginning of the God in me loving me, as God, in my healing journey to becoming One with Love. This is what any healing is ultimately for.

I had never ridden a two-wheeler bicycle in my life, yet I always secretly wanted to. Somehow when this love arose, it seemed important to me that I did this. So, one of the things this heady love for me made me do, was to buy an amazing luminous pink mountain bike, and I tried to learn how to cycle. I never became that proficient at it, but the love I felt for myself was so strong that I had to give myself this opportunity. The cycling and the mountain bike were part of my medicine and healing.

This love has never gone away, although the initial giddiness eventually disappeared. That adolescent-type love has matured into a deeper self-confidence and self-respect for myself, not as an ego, not even as a personality, although they are included in Unconditional Love, as part of God, as Divine. This love has taken years to mature, and is still unfolding. Like all love, it is tested and sometimes its opposite almost wins. Sometimes, I wonder how I could ever have even felt the way I am writing about now.

But, the seed of self-acceptance, self-understanding and desire for Oneness with the Divine was sprouted at this time and it has grown and matured and I trust this love. I trust this love because I know that it sprouted because of God's love for me. And I know that this love has been essential for my healing and the development of my love for God.

I have since met and worked with many people who have not known what I am talking about here. But, I have been privileged to help and witness some, who through their determination to HEAL, have learned to express tenderness and patience towards themselves, and in their efforts to HEAL themselves they have found this love within them also. This is the love of healing towards Wholeness. It is a Divine Force.

I Am You and You Are Me !

The next time I felt this heady love was when I experienced intense bliss for days after a spiritual opening, while on my first pilgrimage in India. It felt like the second chapter of my Divine Love expressing Itself. I awoke feeling Love, Being Love and seeing Love everywhere and in everything. As I looked at the stars in the sky I was in love. There was no division and no duality. The stars were not separate from me. They were me, and I was in love with this wondrous me.

As I was in this bliss I met a leper woman who came towards me, being pushed in a wheel barrow by a leper man who was less handicapped than she. At first, she looked like a bundle of laundry. As the wheel barrow came closer, I saw her condition. Her extremities were either absent or partially there. Because I was in bliss, the sight of her did not affect me. I could see her True Self—beyond the Maya and I felt rapture at the sight of her.

When she saw the joy in my eyes as I looked into her eyes, she extended her bits of arms to me in an embracing unity. Her face burst into an expression of complete happiness. She became as radiant as the sun, reflecting how I felt.

I will never forget the expression in her bright brown eyes. It was Pure Love. She was me and I was her. And we were both in bliss. As we looked into each other's eyes and souls, we were both in love with the other. I was in love with the me in her, and she was in love with the her in me. This is LOVE. This is the unity of Divinity. This is a glimpse of Oneness. This is a glimpse of who we really are and the end of the journey of our healing to Wholeness.

But there are so many of us who still need to connect to this healing force of love and the commitment to find it. Self-healing creates the means to this discovery. But, although some people may accept the idea of self- love, the idea of self-healing is not so easy for their minds. We have got into the habit of thinking that we are helpless and that we cannot help ourselves. We can willingly hand ourselves over to physicians of all kinds, listen to numerous people giving us advise, yet at the same time abandon any sense of our own power and potential to help ourselves. But as well as taking any external help, if appropriate—and many times it is wise and sensible to do so, we can at the same time, also use our own Divine potential to heal ourselves.

You can use any of the techniques given in Part I of this book as well as those in Part II. Self-healing can include working on your own dreams, Journal Work, as well as prayer and meditation. You can also lay your hands on yourself like a hands-on-healer. It does not really matter which methods you use. What is important is your acknowledgement to yourself that you have an inner Divine voice that you can listen to, and that whilst you can use any help that is needed, the responsibility for your healing is yours and God's alone. And, just as you need sincerity, kindness and care from those others you seek out to help you in your quest, you also need to learn how to have sincerity, kindness and care for yourself.

Some people I have worked with cannot place their hands on their bodies in any act of care or kindness. Some, in fact, detest their bodies. I meet people who hit themselves when they do something wrong or call themselves the most terrible names. *You silly cow*, they will say, or *You stupid bitch.* They will even snarl at themselves. I flinch when I hear this, and sometimes it makes me cry. I cannot bear the hardness, the self-recrimination, and the self-judgement. It is awful that we call each other bad names, but when we do it to ourselves we allow the demons of hate and spite to have full rein over us and to laugh and be joyous. *Why*, I have often wondered, *do we do this to ourselves*? And this question makes me want to know how it ever began.

I heard myself say once, in reply to this inner questioning:

This is how it all began... This is how the world began to be heartless and cruel. It did not begin by one being wounded by another. It began with one's heart becoming hardened to oneself, by the judging of oneself with another, by the comparing of oneself with another and deeming oneself as not being good enough. This is when the ego emerged and split with the Divine. Then, the resulting hardness, cruelty and harshness of this self-dislike, self-mistrust and self-abandonment was extended out onto others...

Because, I have so often found people with such a punishing way of being with themselves, that when I teach any kind of healing practices, I first emphasise self-healing. First **HEAL** yourself. Even if we never *try* to help another being in our lives, if we can help to **HEAL** ourselves, to accept ourselves, to be kind and to not judge or condemn ourselves, then there is actually one less person in the world for God to worry about. This in itself is a great healing event. And the amazing thing is that when we are healed, even if we do not try to help anyone, everyone and everything is affected positively and is healed by our being healed.

A Strong Oak Tree Just Is

A strong oak tree just is... It does not need to uproot itself and go chasing after some beings to shelter under its strong wide branches and full leaves. By just staying where it is, many beings can use it and find safety and shelter in and under it.

But the strong oak tree began as a vulnerable sapling. If it had intensely criticised itself and told itself that it was a useless tree and would amount to nothing, chances are it would not have survived. It would have fulfilled its own prophecy.

This is what we do every time we negate ourselves and tell ourselves that we are useless and do not believe in our potential and God-given power to grow into our full maturity.

There is nowhere to go and there is no one really to help. All is One and all is up to God. But we can take responsibility to assist God in helping ourselves. Remember the saying, *God helps those who help themselves.* There is no point whatsoever in trying to save the world or anything or anyone, if we ourselves are mixed up and confused and do not even like ourselves. We just take that whole bundle like a rucksack on our backs and we empty it on whatever floor we find ourselves—mostly other people's floors!

Most people give themselves a terribly hard time, even in the tiniest ways. If we do this to ourselves how can we expect to have a truly loving heart towards others? For example, how many times have you worn uncomfortable clothing only to say, *Oh, this will do*? How many times have you eaten something that you do not even like, but you do not think you are worth the bother of getting something more palatable? How many times do you think that you are an unworthy person? How many times do you expect to be abused?

The point of self-healing is that you take responsibility with God for your healing. It means that you have the possibility to HEAL yourself. It also means that you can choose where to go for help, for the kindest assistance. For instance, if you choose to see a doctor, it is your right to have the one that is the kindest and best for you.

Meanwhile, you do not necessarily need to hand yourself over to anyone else, except God, to HEAL. When you are healing yourself, you can make the best choices for you. This is important, because if you are a person who has a history of not liking yourself and of allowing others to abuse you, you will probably choose anyone—acting without discernment, continuing your pattern.

When you become softer with yourself, kinder and tenderer, the hard shell around your heart which has been there as a protection, can dissolve away and your love begins to flow to every cell of your being. Here are some ways you can begin to be more loving and healing towards yourself—where you can begin or continue with your own self-healing:

Self-Healing Ways

Each day, spend a few minutes
placing your hands lightly and lovingly
on the top of your head.
Next, move them to your occiput
(the lower back of your head above the neck)
Cradle your head as you would a baby's.
Then move your hands to your heart,

and abdomen.
As you do this affirm,
I am Divine.
Ask God to help your Divinity and Healing Love
to radiate through your hands to your body.

When you have a pain, feel hurt, ache or feel sad,
place your hands on yourself in the same loving way,
and particularly on the part of your body that is hurting.

Whenever you feel tired, if only for a few minutes, stop and rest.

Wear comfortable, attractive and colourful clothes.

Try not to compare yourself with others.

Try not to judge yourself.

Do your best
and know that this is the greatest thing
that you can ever do.

At night, before you go to sleep,
Soothe your body by massaging aromatherapy oil on it,
affirming:
My body is the Temple of my Divinity.
Tell your body that you need it to be healthy and strong.
Tell your body that it is beautiful and doing just fine.
If you have difficulty doing this,
massage your fingers and hands, toes and feet
with the same loving intention.

Whenever you catch yourself feeling angry at yourself
stop immediately.

Tell yourself,
I am doing the best I can,
I am in a deep process of learning,
and I am God's own child.

If you catch yourself attempting to hit yourself,
stop.
And instead,
soothe yourself
and reassure yourself:
I am growing
and
I will know better next time.

When you feel hurt,
physically hold yourself lovingly.
Feel love for you and your hurt from your Heart.
Let yourself rest for awhile
at the feet of
God.

When you feel in pain
know that you are loved,
cherished and held by God.

When you feel angry at someone else,
lovingly remind yourself:
This is because
I am deeply hurt
because of something, someone did to me a long time ago.
Turn to yourself in love,
and let your anger go.

When you are rejected
turn to God

and know without any shadow of a doubt that
God will never reject you.

When someone says something horrible to you
or behaves cruelly towards you
try not to take it personally.
Realise that this is really something to do with them,
that this reveals how they are,
and that it says very little about you.
If you can, feel compassion in your heart for them,
for everyone who has caused you pain
and harmed you.
Also, feel the compassion for you.

HEAL

Eve's Inspiring Story of Self-Healing

Eve, a dear friend, was diagnosed in her 30s as having cervical cancer. She was a single mother of an eight-year-old daughter. Eve was advised to have an operation as soon as possible to remove her womb. Her doctors, family and friends, all encouraged her to do this. Her doctor said that without this operation she would be dead within three to four years.

But Eve, had an inner prompting that this was not the way she could HEAL. Her daughter supported her decision, even at that age saying she would eat the same food in order to support her mother. Eve intuited that her cancer was telling her something profound about the meaning of her life, and that removing her womb was not the answer.

Against all the pressing opinions and pressures from those around her, she refused to have the operation and embarked on a powerful healing and spiritual journey, which transformed her and her life, making it impossible for the cancer to exist in the new environment she created.

She began by changing her diet and lifestyle. She embarked on an intense journey of seeking her True Self through meditation, visualisation, psychotherapy, writing and painting. Eve came to realise that having cancer was not the problem in itself, but in fact it was the key to transformation. She also came to realise that if she fought the cancer she would only encourage the ***destructive dynamic*** *she had created in her being.*

Eve came to understand that as a human being she, as all beings, was already basically good and in a state of health. Therefore, there was no need to fight for health. There was, however, a need for her to get in touch with her true nature so that she could allow herself to BE. She realised that she already was Whole. In this BEING she gained access to and activated her creativity, allowing her inherent nature to have true expression, thus strengthening her sense of Self—moving her towards a new way of being.

She subsequently devised a way of working with others, using meditation and painting as powerful tools to enable them ***to be present*** *in their lives—whatever the circumstances. Presently, Eve is writing a book to illustrate the journey, which for her was a journey back to life—to being alive, to being.*

Having cancer became a blessing for Eve, enabling her to turn a life-threatening illness into a life-enhancing situation.

Eve is now in her 50s. The cancer disappeared and never returned!

Honouring Your Energy

16

*Then God said, "**Let us make human kind in our image, according to our likeness**; and Let them have dominion over the fish in the sea, and over the birds in the air, and over the cattle, and over all the wild animals of the earth, and over every creeping thing that creeps upon the earth..."*

The Holy Bible – Genesis 1—Six Days of Creation

Everything in manifestation is sacred. God created everything in Its own image and likeness. You are created in God's likeness. As well as this likeness, you have God within you. God is the real you.

Sai Baba says:

Converse with God who is in you. Derive courage and inspiration from Him. He is the Guru most interested in your progress. Each will come in his own time, at his own pace, through his own inner urge, along the path God will reveal to him as his own.

You have the opportunity to act as your God-Self everyday. You can feed God through your own mouth and speak as God through your own voice. Your body is the Temple of God. With this understanding, take note of what you say, do and eat. Be aware of what enters your Temple through all of the doorways of your senses—your eyes, ears, nose, mouth and hands.

Since your body is the Temple of your Divinity, how would you feel seeing someone deliberately throw piles of rubbish and muck onto the floor of your Temple? Would you feel shocked? Perhaps you would cry. I imagine that this is how God feels when God sees you throwing rubbish into your mouth...or when God watches you in physically or psychically filthy surroundings or covering yourself with disrespectful garments.

God sees everything, for God is always present in your Temple and you take it everywhere you go. What kind of food are you eating and how are you sustaining and nourishing your body Temple?

Your mind is extremely sensitive and subtle. It receives its energy from food. Food that is pure will enable your thoughts to be pure. Food that is dirty will make your mind dirty.

... Hence a close nexus should be established between the mind and the Prana (life force). As is the food, so is the head. Man's thoughts, desires and aspirations are related to the kind of food he consumes...

Sri Sathya Sai Baba

In Hindu philosophy, the world is seen as being permeated by the Divine in the form of three Gunas (qualities). These are called the *tamasic, rajasic* and *satvic* qualities.

Satvic qualities help us to become more pure and balanced. *Rajasic* qualities deepen our connection to our senses and *Tamasic* qualities make us dull and sleepy.

These qualities are inherent in everything we do, in what we eat, and what we experience though our senses.

For example:

The foods that promote long life and vitality, bodily vigour, health, joy and amiability, which are pleasant to the taste, soft, substantial and satisfying, are liked by Satvic natures.

Bhagavad-Gita—XV11-9

Satvic Food

is raw food,
like nuts and fruits,
sprouted pulses and beans.
Uncooked or half-cooked vegetables
and greens.
Flour, rice
and milk, (in moderation).
These promote spiritual and balancing qualities within you.

The passionate desire foods that are bitter, sour, saline, over hot, pungent, dry and burning. These produce sickness, pain and grief.

Bhagavad-Gita—XV11-9

Rajasic Food

is too salty,
too sweet,
too bitter,
too hot,
too sour,
too spicy
and too odorous.
Alcohol (hard liquor)
and meat.
These promote demonic qualities within you.

Food that is not freshly made, food that has lost its flavour, stale food, and food that has gone putrid, leavings of food and food which is filthy, these appeal to men of tamasic nature.

Bhagavad-Gita—XV11-10

Tamasic Food

is overcooked,
reheated
and food that is kept too long,
processed food like
processed cheese,
food that has too much starch,
or fat.
All unperishable foods.
Fish (said to give dirty thoughts)
and
finally wine.
These promote, dullness, sloth and obesity.

Ask yourself what kind of nourishment you give your body through your eyes. You can also receive *satvic, rajasic* or *tamasic* impressions through your eyes. Cultivate discrimination in what you let your eyes see. Do you see truth, love, goodness, non-violence, for instance, *satvic*? Or do you see lust, anger, jealousy and pride, *rajasic*? Do you see meaninglessness, ignorance or filth, *tamasic*?

What kind of nourishment do you give your body through your ears? Do you listen to Divine and sacred sounds, music, harmony, *satvic*? Or do you allow your ears to be bombarded with disruptive noise, disgusting words, gossip, *rajasic*? Do you listen to the monotonous, background sounds, like the television and traffic, *tamasic?*

What kind of nourishment do you give your body through your nose? If you inhale foul, stale odours you will become sick, *tamasic.* If you inhale pickled or sour smells, these will make you restless, *rajasic.* Or do you wish to inhale sweet and delightful smells that will uplift you, *satvic.* Are you breathing in pure clean air or are you breathing in foul smoke?

What kind of nourishment are you giving your body through your hands? Exercise discrimination. You can use your hands for good or bad acts. Are you helping, *satvic,* hurting, *rajasic* or uncaring, *tamasic.*

What kind of company are you keeping? Is it with lazy, depressed people, *tamasic,* with aggressive, ambitious or harsh people, *rajasic,* or with good and compassionate people, *satvic*? Whoever you keep company with is who you will become. If you spend time with people who are not as pure as you, *a little bit of the soot will fall on you.* If you keep company with spiritually inclined and discriminating people, you also will be like this. If you keep company with those who are only interested in worldly satisfaction and pleasures, you will become like them.

But, no matter how good the company you keep, it is realistic to remember that only God can be your truest and most devoted friend. Ultimately, you can only trust God.

Sai Baba once said in a discourse to His devotees:

Who is a real friend? It is said that a friend is one who helps you when you are in need. What is real help? Is it to help you to go to the cinema?

There are two qualities that a friend should possess. He should be like the sandals that protect the feet and the eyelids that protect the eyes. The eyelids are always guarding the eyes. A true friend is one who always protects you from danger and keeps you safe from evil. The kind of pal that tells you how to get away from the police is not a real friend. A real friend is one who sees to it that right from the beginning you don't get into any kind of trouble by entering evil company and getting lured into committing wrong deeds. You cannot find such a friend in this world, no matter how you seek....

Only God is totally devoid of selfishness and self-interest. God can be called the selfless-Self...

In honouring and respecting yourself, also honour your belongings and sacred items. In the East, it is considered very disrespectful to place Holy literature on the floor. When you think about it, it makes sense. But I have seen this happen many times in the West. I have watched in workshops how a person may write something on a piece of paper that is deeply insightful about him/herself and then place it on the floor, and later he/she or others unintentionally stand on it. In this kind of situation, there is little respect, awareness or honouring of that which is an extension, a manifestation of Divinity.

All our actions, thoughts and deeds have vibrations that affect the energy of our bodies. This, in turn, changes us. Refinement of our actions, thoughts and deeds will lead to our spiritual purification. Honouring what is sacred will increase our humility and devotion. Mindfulness of the sacredness of our actions, thoughts and deeds will lead us to fulfilling our Divinity.

In the honouring of seeming little things you can make great strides in your healing towards Wholeness. For example, when you do any writing such as journal work or writing prayers, respect your work by keeping it safe and clean. If you have an altar or ritual table, place it there when it is not in use, or until you are ready to let it go.

When you finish with any writing that you have done, for example, with unsent letters, burn them and offer them back to God, rather than tearing them up and throwing them in the dustpan!

These things are an expression of your particular energy. So, when you tear up a journal, for instance, and throw it in the dustpan, it is like tearing you up and throwing yourself in the rubbish heap. When you are ready to let something go, and when it feels to be the right time for releasing, burn it, and offer its contents for purification to Divinity asking for further, deeper healing, according to *Thy will and not my will.*

You can do the same with any materials that you may use in a workshop. Honour what you have done, and when the time is right to let them go, burn them and offer them to God, asking for the continuance of your healing.

Sacred photographs and books should be treated with respect. Holy photographs of Masters or Divine Beings should never be torn up and discarded. If you really have no need of it/them, and you do not want to pass them onto someone else, it is better to burn them.

In being aware of these small details, bit by bit you will learn how to master your mind and your senses. These may seem like tiny steps, but they are giant ones of self-mastery and control. And, they are a tremendous help to later, deeper, spiritual exercises you will be doing.

Such simple ways of honouring the sacredness of yourself and life will act as a key to the further opening of your Heart.

Your Body Is a Temple

It is the physical, temporary home of the expression of your Divinity.
Therefore,
you should honour your body as you would a Temple.

Just as you would keep a Temple
immaculately clean and shining,
so should you ensure that your body is treated in the same sacred manner.

Your body needs good food,
clean surroundings
and
loving care
to grow and to mature,
so that
The Cosmic Divine Energies
can emanate through It,
when Divine Timing is ripe.

Every second of your life, every moment you have
is the opportunity,
for Divinity to flow through you,
to connect you with God,
and with the Divinity in all beings and all things.

Every second of your life, every moment you have
can be wasted in idle words, actions and deeds.
Or, it can be spent honouring
this rare God–given opportunity.

Every second of your life, every moment you have
can be used for happiness or sadness.
It is your choice.
What you do with your thoughts,
is perhaps the only choice you have.

Everything you see, touch, taste and smell
belongs to the Divine—
the skies, the earth and the seas,

and everything and everyone that is present within them and on them,
is a miraculous manifestation of You.

Respect and care for everything
as you would a small, pure child,
your books, your photographs, your belongings
and all your sacred items.

Honour all the people around you.
Honour this time, this uniqueness, this everything,
for it can never come again.

HEAL

Honouring Time and Space

17

Time is a manifestation of God. Time is consuming man.
God is the consumer of Time itself.
Therefore you should strive to earn the grace of God.
If you waste time you will forfeit God's grace.

Sri Sathya Sai Baba

Time is Divine. Every moment you have can be frittered away and wasted, or it can be preciously used towards your Healing and Wholeness. Energy is also Divine and acts within time. We as human beings have got into the habit of wasting our inestimable energy and time. We waste our lives and opportunities and we waste God's time. There is only Now, and we are usually either thinking of the past or the future and find no advantage in being in the Now.

No matter what your age is, your time is running out fast. Even if you are fortunate enough to have a long life ahead of you there will come the point when you will be dying. And you might wonder what happened to the time you had. Where did it go and what did you do with it? In retrospect was any of it valid, you will wonder, but then it will be too late.

When Death comes, you may not even have the luxury of a few moments to reflect on these things. Death is always your companion waiting by your side, and It can remove you from life in an instant without any forewarning—according to God's plan.

How many moments do you waste in idle and ridiculous thoughts? How many times have you exhausted yourself by silly chattering and needless socialising? How many times do you find that your focus and intention is on external and worldly aims and ambitions, for the satisfaction of the senses? How much of your time is spent in wallowing in self-pity?

How much of your time is used creatively for the good of others? How much of your time is used in helping others? How much of your time is spent in thinking of others and not of yourself, your own wishes and needs and happiness?

Sri Sathya Sai Baba says:

Wealth once lost can be regained;
a lost friend can be replaced;
a lost wife can be replaced;
a lost land can be recovered;
but the Time that has gone cannot be recovered.

You are on a path to Wholeness and all your actions can be pure and from the heart. They need not be meaningless and contaminated. If you act from the heart, no action is wasted. Time spent in an awareness of purifying thoughts and using your discrimination, is time preciously spent.

It is a tall order to be aware enough, vigilant enough and especially *pure* (sincere) enough to make all your actions come from the heart and not from the lower mind. In fact the very idea can be overwhelming and you may feel despondent at the very beginning of such an arduous task.

If, like most people, you can get lost in your thoughts and even forget who you are sometimes—what you are doing and what you were doing or thinking an hour ago or even five minutes ago—performing actions from the Heart may seem an impossible task. But it is not impossible to begin to use your discrimination, and to be more mindful. As you do so you may even like it and want to do it more. If you waste 95% of your time, it is better than wasting 100% of your time. You will have gained 5% more of your Divinity!

One helpful way of achieving this is to re-train your mind. Over the years, lifetimes in fact, your mind has got used to being in control of you. It leads you and you follow. ***What you need to do now is train your mind to follow you.*** This can be done anywhere and at anytime.

You can, for example, begin practising as you awake in the morning. At this time the mind is particularly sleepy and more manageable than later in the day. From the moment you are awake and aware, try being vigilant about your thoughts, actions and deeds. When the mind wants to wander off track and remember all kinds of irrelevant or troublesome thoughts, bring your awareness back to *you and to the now* and consciously think of something positive and good.

Similarly, do the same with your actions and words. As the day progresses, you can still practice discrimination and vigilance. Try, as much as possible to stay quiet internally and externally. Try this for short periods until you feel confident in extending the duration. It is one way of you being really present to your time, and of respecting your energy. There will, of course, be times when it is necessary to speak and communicate with others—particularly in your work place. But when you do speak, try to be aware of what you are saying. Is it necessary? Is it wasteful? Is it appropriate? Will it hurt? Will it help? When you are in doubt, ask yourself the following:

Will what I have to say improve upon the silence?

Sri Sathya Sai Baba

This way of monitoring can be introduced to the lower mind bit by bit, in little ways and even in conversations with people. *Training the lower mind to serve you and not control you is a bit like training a three-year-old child to behave.*

Speaking is a way of losing energy, and so speech should be carefully and respectfully used. This applies to quality as well as quantity. One can get high, can receive energy when talking of Divine stories, and feel elated and Whole. At such times, in fact, one may well not want to stop talking. Compare this, however, to the more trivial and so-called polite and unnecessary conversations we are used to having. We talk about the weather, other people's personal matters, wars, conflict, illness, taxes, what the neighbours are doing, how someone else has a new car, what the cost of that new car might be, and so on. If you really examine the difference, you will realise how quickly your life-force energy begins to drain away within a short time.

The Sacredness of the Cycles of Time

For everything there is a season, and a time for
every matter under heaven:
A time to be born, and a time to die;
A time to plant, and a time to pluck up what is planted;
A time to kill, and a time to heal;
A time to break down, and a time to build up;
A time to weep, and a time to laugh;
A time to mourn, and a time to dance;
A time to throw away stones, and a time to gather stones together;
A time to embrace, and a time to refrain from embracing;
A time to seek, and a time to lose;
A time to keep, and a time to throw away;
A time to tear, and a time to sew;
A time to keep silence, and a time to speak;
A time to love, and a time to hate;
A time for war, and a time for peace.

The Holy Bible—Ecclesiastes 3.1

Attempt to attune yourself to the sacredness of the cycles of time. There are specific energies and vibrational qualities to each day of the week, each week, each month, each season, each year and even to the ages. When you attune yourself to the energies and vibrational qualities of these cycles, you more easily gain empowerment, harmony, balance and protection on all levels of your being.

I have observed that disturbed, stressed or sick people often cannot sleep at night and they are tired during the day. In their disharmony, they are out of tune with the natural rhythm of the world. Normally, we sleep at night and are awake during the day. In slowly adjusting to a normal rhythm, people begin to HEAL and they connect with more of their essential life force for their healing.

It is not by coincidence that ancient teachings tell us not to begin new ventures, plant crops even, when the moon is waning. Magnetic field energies are low then and the vitality needed is not available. When the moon is waxing, up to the full moon, the energies for growth are more easily at hand. Why go against the flow, when you can be empowered and aided by going with the flow?

Similarly, when people tell me that they cannot connect to their spiritual natures or meditate or pray because of the activity of their minds, I have told them to try getting up earlier in the morning. The time between 4 a.m. until 8 a.m. is a naturally good time to meditate and pray, as you will see. Those who have been able to do this have experienced surprising good results. This is because they attune themselves to the perfect timing that Divinity has already provided. When we observe these timings and cycles, we immediately gain the benefit of their built-in Divine magnetic power.

I also know people who have felt upset because they awoke each morning at 4 a.m. They felt bad because they thought that they should be sleeping at this time and that there was something wrong with them. When I explained to them how they were reacting in complete harmony with their spiritual nature, they of course felt good about it, relaxed and now enjoy this time in the morning for contemplation, meditation, healing or prayer. Some tell me that when they awake, they spend around an hour like this, snooze again for another hour and then awake again for the day.

From ancient times, Hindu teachings, for instance, describe cycles of the Epochs; macro aspects of time conceived in the form of Yugas that eternally repeat themselves. These are:

The Kritha Yuga, where Dharma (righteousness)
is the base of life and is sought after.
Followed by,
the Thretha Yuga where God is installed in the heart,
and is sought after.
Followed by
the Dwapara Yuga where friends and relatives are more

sought after than God.
Followed by
the Kali Yuga, where we find ourselves now and where food and the satisfaction of the senses are of the utmost importance.

Although the Yugas signify great time spans, distinct from one another in terms of moral and spiritual life, at a micro level they can be found within our minds. We can enter in and out of each state in any given day. Being mindful of this possibility can make you more vigilant as to how you are spending your time.

You were introduced to *satvic*, *rajasic* and *tamasic* qualities in the previous chapter. These are also good analogies for Yuga states of mind. For example, Krita is a *satvic* state of mind, Thretha is a mixture of r*ajasic* and *satvic* tendencies, Dwapara is a mixture of *rajasic* and *tamasic* qualities and Kali is predominantly *tamasic*. We move in and out of these mind states throughout the day, according to our moods and emotions.

Similarly, these sacred cycles of time and the rhythms in our days can be identified according to periods of hours; and time can be seen in relation to the three Gunas—balanced, equal-minded *satvic*, over active, passionate, *rajasic* and dull and inactive *tamasic*. For example:

Daily Cyclic Rhythm

Satvic
4.00 a.m. to 8.00 a.m.

Rajasic
8.00 a.m. to 4.00 p.m.

Tamasic
8.00 p.m. to 4.00 a.m.

From 4 a.m. to 8 a.m. our minds are still inactive and so our spiritual energies are more accessible to us. Evening and night is a time to slow down, to be quiet and to rest and sleep. From, 8 a.m. to 4p.m., we generally use the more rajasic qualities of our minds at work and in worldly life.

The days of the week, the months, the seasons all have sacred energetic meaning. Attuning yourself to the harmony of Nature and the cycles of time will enrich your own vitality and life force. Autumn is a time to begin to let go in the preparation for the coming winter and stillness. Winter is a time to retreat, to allow your being to integrate the energies you absorbed in Spring and Summer. Spring is when Nature and we feel as though we are coming into new life, re-birth and rejuvenation.

Astrological cycles are not only related to the months of the year, giving particular qualities, but the days of the week are also related in this way. For example, Monday was traditionally known as *the day of the Moon.* Tuesday is the day of Mars, *the day of Honour and Valour.* Wednesday is the day of Mercury, *the day of Wisdom and Communication.* Thursday is the day of Jupiter, *the day of the benevolent God Jupiter and of Spiritual Strength.* Friday is the day of Venus, *the day of Love.* Saturday is the day of Saturn, *the day (of reckoning, or Karma).* And, Sunday is the day of the Sun, and is traditionally the first day of the week and *a time of rest, reflection and worship.*

I have been taught by Indian Hindu women about the relationship between particular Deities to the days of the week and colour. I have found that this can vary in different states and locations. But I like to observe what I was taught. You will note how with many of the days, there is a similarity of energy between the Western and Eastern general descriptions. For instance, Tuesday, in the West, is related to Mars and to valour and honour. In Hindu tradition, it is often related to Hanuman, (Monkey God) with the qualities of courage and devotion. Here are the Hindu descriptions I know:

Monday—the day of worship to Shiva, the God who destroys the barriers of the heart and of the bondage of ignorance. Although He is impulsive and destroys, Shiva is benevolent and bestows boons. In His benevolent state, He can also sometimes be called the Lord of

Sleep, the remover of pain. (Pain is dulled in sleep.) Shiva is also called Nataraja, the God of Dance, and The Cosmic Dancer, who vibrates the entire Cosmos with His movement. On these days I usually wear Himalayan clear-sky blues.

Tuesday—Ganesha and Hanuman day. All ceremonies and rituals begin with invocations to Ganesha. He is the Elephant God, son of Parvati and Shiva, who is the God of Intelligence and the Remover of Obstacles. Hanuman is the Monkey God who was the chief devotee of Rama. (Avatar). He is the Deity of strength, courage and devotion. The sacred colour I was advised to wear on this day is shades of pink to red.

Wednesday—Krishna (Avatar) day. Krishna evokes devotion (bhakti) as a means to becoming One with God. Krishna, from being a small baby until he left His body, charmed his devotees with His bliss and elusiveness. He is often depicted as a sweet infant with a crown of peacock feathers on his head, or as the Divine Enchanter with the Gopis and Gopikas, (bhakti Cowherds) longing to dance with Him (to become One with Him). On this day I like to wear peacock blue/green.

Thursday—Guru day. This day is in honour and celebration of your personal Guru. My Guru is Sri Sathya Sai Baba. He wears an orange robe, and so on that day I also wear orange. Guru day is a day when offerings of flowers, or of actions such as fasting are often done more than on any other days for your Guru. It can be a day that is in honour of all one's teachers in form. But our ultimate Guru is, of course, God.

Friday—Devi (Goddess) day. The Divine Mother. There are three main aspects of the Goddess in Hindu Tradition. Saraswati, consort of Brahma, representing the past and the colour black. Lakshmi, consort of Vishnu, representing the present and the colour red. And, Parvati, consort of Shiva, (representing the future and white). But, Devi, is the mother of all the Goddesses of the Universe. She is the Shakti (energy and power) of the Cosmos, and is the creative aspect of Divinity. She manifests as one of the consorts of Shiva.

This is an auspicious day for prayer for a good marriage, for fertility, or for the healing of afflictions. She is the giver of supreme bliss. On this day I wear earth-green colours to honour Mother Earth or the specific colours of her daughter Goddesses.

Saturday—Ganesha and Kali. Ganesha is referred to in detail on Tuesday's description. Kali, is the aspect of the Devi, which is the female form of time. She is the Beginning and the End. She is usually depicted as wearing a necklace of skulls signifying how she supports the living and the dead. Her colour is black, like the void she is so completely at home with. She is totally without fear. She is the Power of Time and timing. On this day, it is good to wear deep, dark colours or black.

Sunday—Parvati is an aspect of the Great Mother Goddess, Devi. She is also the Goddess of Light and Beauty. Unlike some other Goddesses, she has no tradition of followers, as she is always worshipped with Shiva, her consort. Although she has independence of spirit, she is inseparable from Shiva, and it is their union which manifests life as Consciousness and Enlightenment. On this day I like to wear white or violet in honour of Parvati's purity and of the snow-capped mountain peaks of the Himalayas and of Mount Kailash where Shiva and Paravati are said to reside.

A participant asked me in a recent workshop, when I thought people on a spiritual path would stop bothering about the outer body, clothes and appearances. She had the idea, perhaps, that as we go further into our spirituality we need to renounce and give up the idea of feeling that our outer body appearances are important. I told her that I felt this was a personal choice, whether to become a renunciant or not. It is not essential, but a matter of preference and more suited to some people than others. As for myself, I explained, that I did not think I ever would.

In fact, I had made an effort to look good that day. I had taken some thought about what to wear, was wearing make-up and jewellery. I told her why I did this. *I dress for God* and *I am aware that other people have to look at me.* She laughed and I explained a little to her of why I felt like this.

My dressing for God became a ritual when I began attending the Darshan of Sri Sathya Sai Baba. I observed that He was always freshly washed and dressed in a clean and beautifully simple orange gown. He made that effort for us, and so I was aware that as I dressed for Darshan, I wished to make that effort for Him. But then, God is everywhere, and so I wished to celebrate the Goddess in me and to *dress for God* and particularly when working or being in formal company.

Therefore, when I wear a sari to go to Darshan, I generally choose the colour to wear from the list above. I personally find that it enhances my awareness of the qualities of the particularly powerful spiritual energies for that day, and I often receive confirmation in some form or another. For example, on a Tuesday when I was crossing an open field, contemplating about Hanuman's deep devotion and courage, while wearing a red sari, a monkey appeared as if out of nowhere and ran across the field towards me. It was a little frightening. But then, when he reached me, he looked at me and then passed me. Nothing is by chance, and I felt this to be a personal acknowledgement to me of my actions, prompted by Hanuman Himself.

Your Sacred Space

Just as cycles of time have a spiritually magnetic force of energy *from which you can drink*, the same thing will happen when you ***create your own sacred space***. In time, the Divine magnetic field will build, so that as soon as you enter your sacred space you will feel immediate healing, peace of mind and the correct conditions to meditate, to be still, to receive Divine guidance and inner prompting and to be renewed.

The space need not be large. A small room or corner of a room can be your sacred spot. This can be outdoors as well. You can make a small shrine, altar, or ritual table and place on it what are, for you, sacred and holy objects, photographs and items. Here you can light a candle or incense, burn sage for purification, pray, place letters to God, unsent letters to rectify relationships and names for absent healing. You may place symbols representing your life traumas and wounds in order for them to be healed. You can also place crystals, flowers, stones, feathers, leaves, or other natural items on your altar—you can be as creative as you wish and there are no rules. ***This is your sacred space and no one else's!***

Such a place enhances your connection to the Divine, to the force of the Spirit within you and all around you. It is like a bodyguard, a protector and a healer. It is a place of refuge, your small Temple where you can go externally or even internally in your mind, when you need to. When you complete a long day of work or a difficult or testing time and go to your sacred space, you will find that it is like the womb of Divinity for you. Here you can rest, let go, just be, pray, meditate, contemplate, chant or even sleep. When you are physically away from your sanctum sanctorum, you can mentally think about it and you will feel its healing and protective energies instantly with you.

Choose your corner, cupboard, small room, large room, cave, cabin, tree house, carefully. Try not to have your sacred space near a television or where there are distractions. Place it where no one can use it, or interfere with it. If you have young children and little space, use a shelf on the wall. Do what makes you happy. However, your sacred space can be enhanced by the direction you choose for it. Generally, for example, the placement of the altar faces the East. Each direction has particular energies.

For example, in shamanic tradition:

The *South* is the place of the *Child*, of innocence, creativity and play and is the colour *red*.

The *West* is the place of the *Void*, of hibernation, retreat, contemplation and just being and is the colour *black*.

The *North* is the place of the *Ancestors and of the Great Spirit*, of the knowledge and wisdom that can be gained from this connection and is the colour *white*.

The *East* is the place of *Illumination*, where we can be inspired and awaken and is the colour *yellow*, of the rising sun.

There is no reason why you cannot have four different altars, or sacred spaces to honour each energy. In leading workshops I have at times given the participants a *Quest or a question* and then invited them to sit in each of the four directions to find guidance, and to HEAL, within each space relating to the sacred directions. Some have been amazed at their discoveries and at the resulting Wholeness of their inspired answers.

Also, your sacred space can be portable and be taken everywhere with you. I have painted four smallish stones to depict the directions and their qualities. For example, I usually paint an eagle's head based on yellow on the stone of the East. On the South stone, I paint the figure of a small child, surrounded by vibrant healing red. On the North stone, I paint white buffalo horns (symbolising the American Indian sacred White Buffalo) on a golden/white background, and on the West stone, a dark retreat of a cave, filled with black space, or a bear paw print (one of the sacred animals of the West).

When I finish painting all four stones, I place them around me in a circle, and sit inside it. I sit for some time with my quest/question until I feel ready and open to receive the answers. I turn, after approximately 10 to 15 minutes, facing each direction with my request for guidance, prayer or healing. In this way, I have often received the help of the four directions and their wisdom. I write a short synopsis of how I am inspired before I move on to the next direction. At the end of the contemplation I have four different aspects of my own wisdom to help me understand whatever I have offered for Truth and to HEAL.

I have had profound personal experiences of the miraculous power and grounding of this kind of healing. The following is an account of one of them.

The Miracle of the Mandala of the Four Directions and the Mayan Crystal Skull

From 1980, I have experienced cycles of energy awakenings (Kundalini Energy). The first one was in 1980 and with this I opened up psychically, as if overnight. But it took around three years for this one to integrate, and when it did I then had other Kundalini experiences. Some were more intense. But after activation of energy settled, I was aware of having more consciousness than before. For example, I understood more clearly the dreamlike quality of our relative reality.

Around 1988/'89, I had a series of strong energy awakenings that were particularly intense. The disruption to my nervous system lasted a few weeks. During this time, I could not sleep and felt waves of energy passing through my body, as though internally burning me. I could not keep still and felt overwhelmed. I was unable to work. I paced the floor for hours at a time. I began painting Mandalas to help HEAL *and contain me. Painting the Mandalas made me feel psychically held, and the intricate work along with the use of colour helped to balance me and keep me focussed.*

But, I was living in the city and my telephone would not stop ringing. I was unable to get the peace and rest I needed. When I went outside, I could hardly bear the vividness of colours and the streams of energy that seemed to bombard me. This came from everything and everyone around me. I could not bear sound either—whether it was people talking, children crying or awful background music that seemed to be everywhere I went.

One night a friend from England spoke with me on the telephone, and being aware of my predicament, she invited me to stay at her home to rest, to be in the garden and to have some quiet. She very kindly offered to look after me. Sue, was a good friend and very sensitive and caring, with a very understanding husband. I knew that this would be good for me and so I agreed to go. She lived in the Midlands of England, in a small, old mining village. Nothing much happened in this quiet town. I knew I would be able to find some peace there.

Within a few days, I had packed a small bag, taking with me one book to read. I had not been able to read anything in the state I was in, but something made me put it in my bag. It was about the sacred directions. I travelled by train and Sue met me at the station. From then on, in Sue's garden and home, I began to recover. I continued painting and I gathered some small stones and made a circle to sit in as I described above. This was a rare treat for me. At home, I had no garden to sit in—and here were no telephone calls for me. I did not have to be available for others! At the end of the week I was feeling much better and planned to return home within a few days.

I felt prompted to take a look at the book I had brought with me. I had recently purchased it and was not aware of all the contents, so I began to scan it. I sat in Sue's garden looking at the book, revelling in feeling so balanced and well again. I was grateful that I could read.

I noticed a chapter on a Mayan Crystal Skull and became interested. I began reading about an amazing rock crystal skull, reputed to be around 3600 years old and which, according to legend, was used by a High Priest of the Mayans when performing esoteric rituals. It was also called the Skull of Doom, as when the Priest used it and wished death on someone the event would follow shortly after. I read how in 1927 a young girl, called Anna, found the skull on her 17th birthday while accompanying her adoptive father on an archaeological excavation of an ancient Mayan City, in Belize.

On that sunny afternoon as I sat in the quiet garden reading Anna Mitchell Hedges' story, the telephone rang in the background and I heard Sue answering. She came to the garden and asked me if I was feeling well enough to be able to go somewhere that evening. She told me that an elderly lady from Canada was staying overnight in a nearby village and asked if I wanted to meet her. To my absolute amazement, Sue said the lady's name was Anna Mitchell Hedges and she had this Mayan Crystal Skull with her and we could meet up if we wanted to…!

We, of course, went. I was astounded. I kept thinking that this was some peculiar cosmic joke and that we would not see the Skull at all. I thought that perhaps what we would see would be a replica. I felt that it could not possibly be the same skull I had just begun reading about. And if it was, what kind of miraculous powers did it have to enable this kind of synchronicity to happen?

The timing was perfect for me, as I am sure it was for Sue. I met Anna Mitchell Hedges and the fabulous Skull and we sat with some other people and meditated with it. I felt wonderful touching it and was awed at its perfect beauty and mobile, detachable jaw. There was, I sensed immense power emanating from it.

It is a perfect copy of a human skull, but is made of the clearest, purest rock crystal. No one understands how the Mayan people could have made the skull. I was told that it was estimated that it would have taken generations of workers, scouring the crystal with sand abrasives, up to 300 years to carve. The roof of the mouth acts as a prism and when light, say a flame, is placed below the skull, the prism projects the light through the eyes. Because the fabrication of the skull seems beyond the capabilities of the Mayan people, many experts believe it to be alien—from another planet.

I asked Miss Mitchell Hedges, who was in her 70s at that time, about her story and she told me how, that fateful morning of her 17th birthday, she saw something glistening beneath rocks while her father was excavating. She showed this to her father, Michael Mitchell Hedges, who then dug it out of the rubble.

The skull has been her almost-constant companion since, and of course has shaped her entire destiny. How we met that evening in this remote village was because she was on her way to London to find out if the British Museum could accommodate a safe place for the skull to be on view and where people could also touch it. She told me that she did not wish it placed behind a closed screen.

I found her delightful and it was a joy to meet her. I was excited to tell her how we received the invitation to meet her just as I was reading her name. She was not at all surprised. She said many, many strange and astounding events were linked with the skull.

I have since heard of many people who wanted to observe the Mayan Crystal Skull and have found it difficult to do so. For some reason, I realised that the skull wished to meet us. How else could this extraordinary meeting have happened?

I have yet to realise the purpose of this meeting. Sue and I guessed that maybe we had been invited because we were both known psychics.

However, to this day we still don't really know why the skull wanted to meet us. What I am acutely aware of, though, even now after these many years, is the integral, synchronistic relationship between my series of energy awakenings, the subsequent powerful healing with the four sacred directions and the stone Mandala, resulting in the spectacular encounter with the Mayan Crystal Skull.

HEAL

Honouring Your Quest

18

The Inner meaning of life does not readily reveal itself; it must be searched for. Such a search is the Quest. When a man begins to seek out his real nature, to find the truth of his real being, he begins to follow the Quest.

The Quest is a veritable re-education of the self, leading in its turn to a noble transcendence of the self. Some come to the truth in a roundabout way. The Quest is direct. The Quest is spiritual mountaineering.

Paul Brunton—
The Notebooks of Paul Brunton, Vol. 2, The Quest

We are all on a continuing Quest—of healing towards Wholeness. Each time we go through a process of healing and we HEAL, we feel the benefits. It is as if we are on a long cruise towards the Divine Harbour and on the way our ship docks at a port for a while. We land on new ground, enjoying looking at the scenery, and taking in the different sounds, smells and tastes. We can enjoy our well being and rejoice in the wonderment of being alive, of feeling good and of being connected to everything.

But why stop here, when we can go back on the ship, journey and explore what else belongs to us? Why should we stop with a temporary holiday, a small island, when we can claim the whole world? Why should we remain with momentary relief and pretend that it is permanent? When we know that we are on a journey towards Wholeness, and that there is no end to it until we become One with All, we will never be limited. We will desire to move on, to explore the depths of The True Self, and in this way we can honour each transition, each moment of healing as a Divine glimpse towards this Wholeness.

Let us take some rest by all means; but know that to stop now will lead us once more up blind alleyways. When we feel increased healing, when we are aware of growing consciousness, we will most probably also have renewed energy and vitality. Let this renewed vital energy take us to deeper healing on all levels. Let us conserve this sacred energy and use it creatively rather than dissipate it.

You can see that it is relatively easy to get help and to learn how to help yourself. There are so many different good methods of treatment and healing. Whatever we need is completely provided for by God from the myriad spiritual teachings, paths, meditations, excersises, books and teachers that can inspire us on our way. We cannot miss out; we cannot miss the boat! Even if the ceiling has to fall in on you, as it once did on me, and the floor has to collapse, before you get the message, God will make sure that you catch the boat and get back home no matter what the obstacles seem to be.

But sometimes we seem to go around in circles and not be able to HEAL.

Healing, in any form, and on any level can happen, sometimes quite dramatically. The effects can stay for some time. (Perhaps even for a lifetime!) But as we already saw in the last section, if our perspective is *limited* and we stop and settle for what is temporary and *worse than second best*, we will fall back again, and one day we will have to go deeper for more permanent solutions. But the fact that you are reading this book indicates that God already has enlarged your Spiritual Vision.

So now that you are on ***The Quest***, that Paul Brunton so aptly described as ***Spiritual Mountaineering***, be aware that there are some dangerous spots on the mountain that you can avoid. They are:

Dissipation of New Energy, Misuse of Increased Vitality, and a Return to Old Habits.

Dissipation and Misuse of Precious Life-Force Energy

But he is worthy who controls the senses by his mind,

uses his organs of action without developing attachment towards sense-objects, and thus practises the Yoga of action.

***Bhagavad-Gita*—III-7**

Often, when people get renewed energy through having less pain, the gaining of some wish, or an increase in consciousness because of a spiritual breakthrough, they feel high and they lessen the activities that helped them with the breakthrough. They feel so good that they re-enter life with renewed vigour.

With an increase in well being, we can be tempted to talk non-stop, hurry here and there, party, socialise, eat erratically and sleep too little. Meanwhile the newfound energy and good health is quickly dissipated. Some even put all their energy into making a fortune, (which is not a bad thing) but if it is at the expense of spending most of their valuable life-force energy working with little time for anything else, it can have long-term devastating effects. Usually, when we do this, the first things shelved are the spiritual or inner practices that got us started.

Of course, these energy expansions can also be psychic rather than physical, but the pitfalls are the same. My own increase in understanding of this vital-energy dissipation happened through trial and error. But through my rather painful experiences and what I learned, I have since been able to help others to not fall into the trap as I did. I had no sense at all that my energy could in any way dry up or that it was limited.

I had an initial, huge psychic opening around 1980, which gave me tremendous psychic energy—for about seven years. During this time, I was able to do just about anything I psychically tried, demonstrations of clairvoyance, trance work, channelling and so on. As well as being available to people for readings and healing, I taught Psychic Development in the evenings, while working during the day as a Government Officer. I had a home to run and was a single mother. I never stopped! I did not even think about it. Neither did I pay any attention to my diet, which was erratic, and consisted of what I know

now to be all the wrong foods. And I was a chain smoker. During my lunch times I even went to the gym to lift weights. I did not know what it was to rest, to contemplate or to just be. I was addicted and attached *to doing*.

Of course, this could not go on and eventually I plummeted into ill health. I really did fall off the mountain. Interestingly, I did not lose my psychic abilities, but I became seriously and chronically ill with M.E. (Chronic Fatigue Syndrome). I could hardly walk at times. I could barely exist and I realised that I had no energy left from which to draw. I had used up everything I had, and there were no reserves left. I was burned out. I wondered if I would ever be able to recover. It was only then that I realised the preciousness and the limitations of our energy on every level of our beings. I had to fall that far to find this out.

I had to dig deeper within myself to find another wellspring of energy. Fortunately, I was blessed in that it was not too late and I found one. But it took a lot of effort. For approximately five years, I entered into intense self-development and healing, studied Dream Work, psychoanalysis and spiritually searched. As I did this, I became well again, and my energies renewed. This foundation became the basis for my deeper and ongoing spiritual search that preceded these five years and which led me to India. But, I now honour and observe my energies in a way that I could not possibly have done before. Even so, to this day my nervous system is fragile. I have learned and I am grateful to have been given the opportunity to do so, but it has been at tremendous cost. Hopefully, some of what I say here can help you not to be so foolishly blind as I was.

I find that when we experience an expansion, then a strong contraction through misuse of energy, we can become worse off than before. If this happens, we enter a dark night of the soul. We complain that we are tired and unwell, we question the healing, we question the journey, we question God and we question whether or not there was ever a Quest! We become disillusioned—spiritually, emotionally, mentally and physically.

Every expansion is followed by a contraction. This is normal. For instance, if you have an increase in consciousness that makes you feel elated, or at one with everything, even if for a moment, it is likely that within a few days you will experience a corresponding depression. It's a bit like an elastic band. We also are like tight elastic bands in our limited consciousness. When we have experiences of expansion, it is as though we are elastic bands that are pulled and stretched. Suddenly there is an expansion and we feel unrestricted. But then we are let go of and we snap back into our former shapes. However, we can never be the same again. We may look the same, but, like an elastic band, we are looser and each time this happens we become more slack and pliable. Eventually we can become so stretched that we break. In this way, we are pulled and stretched by God until we break free from the hard binding of our egos.

But when we dissipate and misuse our precious energy, we make the contraction more so and it becomes excruciatingly painful. This is not necessary for us to endure. God's stretching and pulling is enough to endure. When we gain a precious increase in our energies, this can be used for our continuing healing towards Wholeness. Whenever we feel or think that we are separate from God our energy is limited. We have a certain amount of energy in this split, within the confines of our bodies. ***We need energy to move energy and we need energy to increase our energy.*** We need energy to HEAL. We need energy to wake up—to become enlightened! We need energy to become One with God.

If all we do with any expansion of precious energy is continue our old habits with renewed vigour and with our limited and draining ways of being, we perhaps ruin the opportunity of our lifetime. Life, unlike Death, will not wait for us. It will go on with its ups and downs. But if we carry on unconsciously and wastefully during the *good times*, then when we are faced with the challenges and crises that will come later, and our *luck* runs out, we will have nothing from which to draw. It is at these times that we can become chronically or fatally ill. There is nothing left in the wellspring of our life.

Sarah's Meditation Experience—What Not to Do

Sarah made a commitment to learn meditation because she had been feeling stressed and tired. She found it difficult to concentrate and she often felt depressed. She had lost heart in her work and in making any effort to change herself or her life. She did not see much point in doing anything. She had moved house within the last two years and had also experienced an emotional let down, when her boyfriend, whom she thought she would marry, fell in love with someone else and left her.

She came across the idea of meditation in an article as a way of relaxation and to alleviate stress. Even though Sarah felt a bit depressed she was attracted to the idea of meditation, so she joined a local meditation group. This group helped to lead her into basic meditation techniques such as: watching the breath, not following her thoughts and learning how to find some quiet time and space for herself where she could just let go and be.

She decided to get up a little earlier in the morning and spend around 10-15 minutes in meditation before going to work. She did the same when she returned home in the evenings. As well as this, she attended the weekly meditation group for support.

As soon as Sarah first started meditating, she experienced an almost immediate high. This makes sense. Imagine a mind that has been held in thoughts unceasingly for 30 years. Suddenly, for 10 minutes in the morning and 10 minutes in the evening, Sarah's mind got an opportunity to rest a little to have a bit more space. This was a huge relief of pressure. The mind is a bit like a constant pressure cooker. Suddenly, Sarah's mind was able to let off steam two times a day and it felt very good! Sarah's whole body in turn became positively affected by this release and she had more energy. This, in turn, made her emotionally happier and she felt much more able to be open with others and was able to welcome life again.

Now, Sarah continued like this for around three months. She experienced what often happens and with her extra energy and renewed interest in life, she understandably wanted to use it. After all, she had it, so why not use it? But, of course, how she used it determined whether she would continue to increase her healing and well being or begin falling down the mountain.

Sarah did not do anything so drastic or seemingly that bad. She decided to get a part-time job as well as her main job since she wanted to make some extra money. Because she felt so energised and optimistic she thought she could manage this just fine. But then, after a few weeks of this new regime, she began to feel tired again. There was a reason for this—because she was now working quite long hours and she did not have much free time.

She was unable to attend her weekly meditation group but she had told them that she intended to continue with her morning and evening meditation, as it was so helpful to her. But, the extra work and the tiredness made Sarah feel once more lethargic and she soon discontinued with her morning and evening meditation times.

She very quickly deteriorated back to square one! The little increase of energy she had experienced soon dissipated and without continuing her routine to help her with her inner connection and further possible expansions, Sarah plummeted downhill.

When I met her, Sarah was feeling disillusioned with anything to do with meditation and spiritual practices for she said that they did not work and that, in fact, she was feeling much worse than before because of them. She came to me for hands-on healing.

But of course, without an awareness of how to avoid what had happened to her, any energy she received from the healing would be similarly wasted. This was the real issue.

Sarah did get back up the mountain path. We discussed that even if she had not got the extra job, the main issue was that she continues with the practises allowing the energy increases. I explained to Sarah that when we feel good there is usually not the same intensity for us to try. Sarah realised that she could easily fall into this trap again. With some healing and betterment, she might relax from her determination and commitment and want to enjoy her self in the self-destructive ways that had led her to seek external help in the first place. (Know, for example, that the same thing can happen when we first go into any kind of new technique or therapy or find a Guru, or even when we fall in love...)

After some sessions, Sarah realised what had happened to her and she began once more a routine of meditation. She realised that it had helped her. This time she knew how to honour more and respect the benefits she was receiving and Sarah is now continuing her healing towards Wholeness.

You as the Meditator—Doing Well

Imagine you have experienced renewed vitality, as a result of recently taking up some meditation. You feel good, but you realise that you do not really want to dissipate this newfound vitality. And so you decide to just sit on it. You choose not to enter into any new activities, go back to your old bad habits, sleep less than usual, eat erratically and you mindfully do not waste, but conserve your energy.

Initially you feel that you want to buzz around but you resist the temptation because you are interested to see what happens if you do not. With the additional energy you have, you feel inspired to increase your meditation time from 10 minutes to 20 minutes in the morning and 20 minutes in the evening. You feel even greater. You feel sharper, healthier and stronger.

You are aware that you are building reserves in your energy bank. You know this because you do not get tired in the way you did before, and you also are not so affected by the stresses and strains of daily life. When they come, you have the energy to deal with them.

As time goes on, you are aware of deeper healing taking place within you. Your energy centres (Chakras) are becoming more vibrant and you feel much more sensitive and aware. Your insights deepen.

Each day, you feel stronger—emotionally, physically, psychically and spiritually. As more time goes on, you are aware that as you increase your energy, there is more opportunity for further strengthening and increase.

With your additional strength, vitality and awareness you find the will power to change your lifestyle and habits even further. And as you continue this momentum, you experience more and more transformation, and your life changes far beyond what you could ever have initially imagined.

As still more time goes on, you wonder: What next? What might happen for me now?

This could be you. Do not limit yourself, your healing or your journey. If you consider the idea of healing as something to give you mere relief this is most probably what you will get. But if you go for your True Healing, you will increasingly connect with the profoundness of your Self, your Divinity. Here, there is unlimited opportunity available for you to spiritually grow, unfold and **HEAL**.

In the meantime, take note of the following possible traps that can entice you to return to **old habits** and make you tumble.

Our Old Habits

The soul does not attain freedom from action through refraining from activities.
By merely abstaining, one does not attain perfection.

Bhagavad-Gita—III-4

But I Deserve This!

On your journey stay as vigilant as you can. At some point, your ego will try to trick you by tempting you to keep on that old coat. Or, if you have taken it off, will try to fool you into putting it back on again. Yes, you can put it back on again, even if you have taken it off. Your ego will have quietly stored that old coat in some hidden psychic corner waiting for the right moment to give it back to you. It will argue petulantly, *Why should I conserve my deserved healing and energy? Why can't I use it? Why should I have to try to do something that feels like more "work"? I have done enough work and so now why should I not enjoy myself?*

Or, perhaps it will say something like, *I have had to really try to get better and it has been difficult and now I deserve a break!*

Or,
Well, I think that I deserve this now
(a packet of cigarettes and a few glasses of brandy),
or,
We all need a little comfort,
or,
Well I am only human.

Regardless of whether you will get hurt, your ego will want its coat. The important thing for the ego is that its desires be satisfied. If you find you are saying any of these things to yourself, this is what is happening. Your ego is trying to take firm control of you again. That way, your ego will feel safe and secure again with its familiar habitual patterning and pain.

But, it is such a pity don't you think, that we believe, with the help of our egos, that *We are only human?* To be given the chance of a human life is the most fantastic opportunity we can receive from God and this human life is immersed in Divinity. Our human life really does deserve the best.

When we think that we deserve some comfort we need to be mindful as to *What/who is it that wants to be comforted and why?* Usually it is the ego that wants to be comforted. And after you give it the temporary feeling of gratification, it has desired, *What then?*

I have heard myself use some of these excuses (and at the very least I have thought them) especially when it has had to do with my wanting to continue some damaging habit or addiction. I used them when I was addicted to cigarettes. It took me some time to realise that this was the last thing my Divinity—my Consciousness, wanted. I was only listening to and voicing my ego. It was, in fact, the very last thing I deserved! But my ego and its friends of addiction and desire just couldn't bear the thought of doing without.

At certain stages in your development, just one tiny drop of alcohol or cigarette smoke or even animal flesh can pollute your astral body, and your other subtle vibration bodies (those energies reflected by your Aura) for months—even years. This in turn will cloud your ability to be increasingly conscious. Doing these things or not, is a matter for your Conscience and between you and God. Not everyone, for example, feels well being vegetarian or vegan. No one can tell you what is right for you. But certainly your Conscience, your ***Divine Telephone***, is a good indicator and is directly linked to God.

But usually when you are meant to let something go it lets go of you. It is at this time, that you need to take notice and act upon your inner prompting. When/if it is appropriate for you to give anything up, God will provide the inspirations and means for you to do it.

I now no longer smoke cigarettes, drink alcohol or eat flesh (anything that has a potential face)! You may recall my being able to give up cigarette smoking in the Self-Love Chapter, through Divine help. I know, however, that I might still be having an occasional glass of wine and eating fish and chips, if it had not been for Sai Baba's strong prompting, through synchronicity, teachings and dreams. Once I heard Him give a discourse, in which He said,

If only you would do three things for me—don't smoke, don't drink alcohol and don't eat animals...

Because of my devotion for Him, I was surprised at how easily I was able to obey His instructions, without feeling that I was missing anything. The desire just fell away. Also, I was and still am aware that this is what He deemed for me, but that this is not necessarily what is spiritually good for everyone. I do know of some people who do not wish to stop eating meat, who cannot, for example, and Sai Baba has personally told them that it is okay.

I say to people who ask me about this not to try to force yourself to do anything, for this just makes a strong contraction and most probably a resulting, catapulting back into what you are trying to strain away from. If in doubt, ask God. Pick up the ***Divine Telephone*** and connect with your Conscience. God will let you know what you are to do, if you are to give anything up, or even whether it is good for you.

But try to stay with your commitment to not fall into your desires and sense satisfactions whatever they may be. An overshadowed and dimly lit consciousness that is clouded by sense satisfaction and desires makes us lethargic and weak. It gives us the feeling that we ought to put off our self-connection and healing until tomorrow. Well, tomorrow may never come. Tomorrow we may die. What then?

Is it not a waste to go to sleep on your permanent Divinity for the temporary satisfaction of an impermanent desire? You can ask yourself, if what the ego is trying to get you to do is really what you deserve or need? It is in this kind of questioning that you can become more discriminative.

Astral Smoke

After I was finally able to stop smoking with Divine help (See the Chapter on Self-Love.) I was aware at times that I was smoking in the astral realms during sleep. Over a period of approximately seven years I remembered a few dreams where I was smoking and feeling satisfied. Yet, externally, I could not now even bear the smell of a cigarette and had no conscious desire to smoke again. I realised, however, that although I had externally kicked the habit, my subtle body was still addicted and needed to satisfy the urge to smoke.

Finally, one night, I was aware of dreaming. I subtly knew that I was dreaming but remained in the dream and asleep. I knew that my astral body (psychic desire body) was due to finally let go of the habit of smoking—that it was the time to now do this. But just before this final letting go it really wanted to break out and satisfy itself.

I recall that I had at least three cigarettes in my mouth, and I was trying to smoke them all at once. I had never been so desperate before! I remember puffing and inhaling the smoke as much as I could. It was as though I could not get enough.

Suddenly, I was aware of Sai Baba walking towards me and I felt like a naughty child caught in the act of doing something wrong. I hurriedly put all the cigarettes out. I felt frantic to get rid of them and hide the evidence.

I stood, as if to attention, looking perfectly innocent and as though I had been doing nothing at all.

Sai Baba came near to me and looked intently into my eyes. "Have you been smoking?" He asked. His question proved that He knew, but I still wondered if I could get away with a denial. I felt so guilty to have been smoking. I was aware of a fleeting thought passing through my mind, as I looked back into His eyes. Is there some way I can get out of this, I wondered? But, I knew that I could not. I had to be honest and face the consequences, whatever they might be. And so, I looked back at Him, staring squarely into His eyes and said, "Yes."

My Guru smiled and walked on. As far as I am aware, I have never smoked on the astral level since. My astral body was also cured of the habit, with the help of the Divine.

You too, if/when you wish, can have any help you need or desire from the Divine. It is only a question of asking, of feeling ready for the next step. The support and help you need will be there for you. Don't give up, or get discouraged if your healing is not overnight or according to your plan. God has perfect timing and knows exactly what you need and when.

As well as these obvious attachments and addictions, you can have more subtle ones, and you need vigilance to catch these too. But once you get into the new habit of witnessing them, rather than enacting them, it can even be fun! For example, watch out for one I know well, which is, It's not fair.

When I buy into this belief I assume that if I am a good person and do my best, then I should always feel good and my life should be relatively easy. I have sometimes assumed that if I *am good*, life will be good to me and if I am very, very good, and do everything fairly and honestly then I will get the same back. But, this attachment has at times almost made me ill with despair. Because life is just not like that.

After a series of shocks when people were incredibly abusive to me, and when I felt that I had done nothing to deserve what was happening to me, I was Divinely inspired to look around me and to find if anyone had missed out on what was happening to me. True enough, in some form or another, life was not being *fair,* nor had it ever been fair to anyone I knew.

Try what I did, and find out if you get the same or a different answer. Try to find someone who has never had anything seemingly unfair ever happen to him/her. If you cannot find someone, anyone in the world who has not had this problem, then you might feel as I began to—that *it is foolish to hold onto the attachment of how I feel the world should be.* You can instead cultivate a belief similar to the following:

There is such a thing as fairness,
but it is not always as I see it—
nor in the terms of my limited sense
of understanding and timing.

This would seem to be more realistic.

Who, Me?

Our acts are all determined by the propensities of our nature.
The illusion of the ego makes the individual consider itself the doer.

Bhagavad-Gita—III-27

What precipitates another potential tumble off the mountain is when we balk at the idea of having to *do it* ourselves! There is sometimes something magical about letting another take the responsibility for *our* healing. We rather someone else *do it* for us. It is quite amazing how much trust we do put into others' ideas and opinions. Through internally negating our self-power, control and responsibility we most probably got into trouble in the first place.

When we are desperate we will usually go anywhere, do anything and trust anyone ELSE, rather than look to ourselves. We ignore the Divine Managing Director, try to step down from the post of Manager, and we hand the whole *liability* over to workers and helpers! This of course leaves us free to get angry with them and not ourselves when it does not work out! It also allows us to be victims.

When I think that the going is getting tough, when I find that I have lost my energy, that nothing is going according to plan, I try to realise that what is happening to me is due to something I have done, am doing, expecting or precipitating—either in the now or in the past. I tell myself that I need to understand that no one is **doing it** *to me. Rather, what is happening to me is a consequence of my own thoughts, words or deeds. Not only that, these consequences may be so old as to have stemmed from a previous lifetime(s) and are my Karma.*

But, because I set the wheels in motion, I can stop them. How do I do that? I realise that I need to change my thoughts, words and deeds that are causing the wheels to turn in this way. This is my responsibility to myself—to look at my habits, my patterning of thought, words and speech and to remove those old coats I am still wearing. My first responsibility is to pray to the Doer of all things, to God, to help me in my quest for understanding and healing and to bless me that I will succeed,

according to Thy will and not my will, and for the good of all concerned.

The development of our taking responsibility for our pain and healing is a tremendously healing act in itself. Here, we cannot hold onto bitterness or resentment. Ultimately, there can be no blame on anyone or anything else for our suffering. But then neither should we blame ourselves. Whatever we have done, whatever we do, we cannot do without God's will, God's allowing.

Everything that happens has to do with our, and everyone else's, growing and understanding. And we can only do our best, to the best of our knowledge at any given time. Harbouring feelings of guilt will not help us. However, our new healing attitude accepts the taking of self-responsibility *for our healing* with an acknowledgement that we can be more conscious. We can HEAL.

Why Me?

As smoke surrounds the fire, as a mirror is covered with dust,
As the embryo is encased in the womb,
the understanding is enveloped by this enemy (illusion).

Bhagavad-Gita—III-38

The *Why me*? question is similar to the *Who, me*? question. If you believe that everything happening to you is a result of God's will and your own actions, at some point in time, and that it is a part of your very own unique way of growing from ignorance to understanding, through healing to Wholeness, then you cannot say, *Why me?*

These kinds of questions will not only make you feel as if you are a sorry victim, but also make you bitter and resentful. With this kind of attitude you can never experience any real change or maturity. What is required is an acceptance of life is as it is now. Everything, even the pain, is a gift. Nothing then is a punishment.

We sometimes see Karma, as something retributive, but it is not. God is not looking to punish us. Our Karma, however, is a means to our becoming more aware, more conscious, through the trials, the tests and the awareness of the patterning. We are undergoing experiences that are the result of previous actions and being given a chance to grow, and form and to redo our earlier scripts. They give us a chance to transform. We do not need to say, *Why me.*

We can say,

I am happy it is me!

With this awareness (consciousness), your Karma (ignorance) actually has a chance to leave you and you have already changed!

Poor Me !

It is said that this enemy seizing the senses, the mind and Reason

and thus closely surrounding and isolating the understanding
uses them to bewilder the soul.

Bhagavad-Gita—III-40

If we say or believe in being *Poor Me*, we once more see ourselves as victims and life and the world is *something that is being done to us*. Self-misery and self-centredness are main obstacles to our growth. We need to identify these ego tricks of the mind and get past the feelings, *let go, forgive, accept and hope.* Only our egos can be happy in *self-centred old coats*, wallowing in their own misery. Only our egos can actually be comfortable and reassured by such feelings. This is a good way for our egos to escape.

But do *you* want to be an escapist? Or do you really want to be Divine?

Letting Go of the Poor-Me Feeling

How can I feel wholehearted and generous towards others?
How can I accept my part in everything and then be able
to change if necessary?
The seeds of Karma are –
As you think, so you shall become,
and,
as you sow, so you shall reap.

If you feel sorry for your lot throughout your life you will continually reap the seeds of misery. If you change your thoughts and attitudes and welcome what comes to you with an accepting Heart, the happiness will come back to you. ***Every thought has energy, a colour, and a form, a reaction and a result.*** It is these vibrational waves that shape our lives. It is these propensities which become our masters, and which we become slaves to, or which we ourselves can master.

Honour Your Quest

Claim your Birthright.
Accept your Divinity.

Trust your Sacred Journey.
Know that you will reach Wholeness,
your at-one-ment with God,

HEAL

Finally, let us pray :

I bow in front of Thee,
I bow to Thee behind.
Prostrations on every side to Thee, O All.
Of energy boundless, measureless in strength,
Thou art the completion of everything;
Thou art everything Thyself.

Bhagavad Gita–XI-40

Therefore, I fall prostrate and offer salutations to Thee;
worthy Lord, I seek Thy Grace;
Thou shouldst bear with me as father does with son,
as friend with friend,
as lover with his beloved.

Bhagavad Gita—XI-44

Credits

We gratefully acknowledge the publishers of the following sources:

1. How You Can Talk to God by Paramahansa Yogananda, Self-Realization Fellowship, California, USA, 1981, 2000.
2. Inspired Thoughts by Swami Rama, Honesdale, PA, The Himalayan International Institute of Yoga Science and Philosophy of the USA, 1983.
3. Man and His Symbols by Carl G. Jung, Aldus Books 1965.
4. Meditation in Action by Chogyam Trungpa, Shambhala, Boston, MA, 1998.
5. Scientific Healing Affirmations by Paramahansa Yogananda, Self-Realization Fellowship, California, USA, 1981.
6. Songs of Enlightenment—Poems of Swami Rama Tirtha translated from the Urdu and Persian by A.J. Alston, published by Shanti Sadan, London. www.shantisadan.org
7. The Dalai Lama's Book of Wisdom by H.H.The Dalai Lama, Thorsons, An Imprint of Harper Collins Publishers, London, 1999.
8. The Essence of Self-Realisation by Paramahansa Yogananda, Self-Realization Fellowship, California, USA, 1981.
9. The Notebooks of Paul Brunton by Paul Brunton, Vol. 2, The Quest, Burdett, NY: Larson Publications, 1986.
10. Dream Yoga and The Practice of Natural Light by Namkhai Norbu Rinpoche and edited by Michael Katz, Snow Lion Publications, Ithaca, NY, USA, 1992.
11. The Prophet by Kahil Gibran, Rupa &Co., India 2002.
12. The Supreme Yoga, A New Translation of the Yoga Vasishta,

Vol. II, translated by Swami Venkatesananda, by The Divine Life Society, U.P. Himalayas, India, 1995.

13. The Tibetan Book of Living and Dying by Sogyal Rinpoche, Rider, London, 1992.

14. The Truth Is by H.W.L. Poonja, VidyaSagar Publications, San Anslemo, California, 1995.

15. Walking Between Two Worlds, The Way of Compassion by Gregg Braden, c/o Radio Bookstore Press, WA, USA, 1997.

Suggested Reading

1. Be Happy with Prayer, Meditation and Affirmation by Mynavati, Tiger Moon Productions/Cosmic Power Press, India, 2002, cosmicpowerpress@yahoo.co.in
2. Gods and Goddesses of India by Anjula Bedi, Eeshwar, India.
3. Hands of Light: A Guide to Healing Through the Human Energy Field by Barbara Ann Brennan, Bantam 1987.
4. Kundalini Yoga by Swami Shivananda, (Shivananda Nagar), The Divine Life Society, 1971.
5. Memories, Dreams and Reflections by Carl G. Jung, Harper Collins, 1983.
6. Maharishi's Gospel, The Teachings of Sri Ramana Maharishi, Sri Ramana Ashram, Tiruvannamali, India, 1999.
7. Sathyam Sivam Sundaram Series (Life Story of Bhagawan Sri Sathya Sai Baba), by Professor N. Kasturi, Sri Sathya Sai Books & Publications Trust, Prasanthi Nilayam, A.P. India.
8. Spirituality and Health by Dr. Mrs. Charanjit Ghooi, Sri Sathya Sai Books & Publications Trust, Prasanthi Nilayam, A.P. India.
9. Sathya Sai Speaks Series Vol. 1-XXVII – Discourses by Bhagavan Sri Sathya Sai Baba, Sri Sathya Sai Books & Publications Trust, Prasanthi Nilayam, A.P. India.
10. The Bhagavad Gita.
11. The Bible.
12. The Dreamwork Manual by Strephon Kaplan-Williams, The Aquarian Press, 1984.
13. The Gospel of Sri Ramakrishna Vol. 1 & 11, by Mahendranath Gupta "M." translated by Swami Nikhilananda, Sri Ramakrishna Math, India.

14. The Medicine Cards by Jamie Sams and David Carson, Bear and Company, USA 1988.

15. The Ramayana.

16. The Truth Is by Shri H.W.L. Poonja, Vidyasager Publications, San Anselmo, California, USA, 1995.

17. The Third Eye and Kundalini (An Experiential Account of Journey from Dust to Divinity) by B.S Goel, The Third Eye Foundation of India, Shri Siddheshwar Ashram, India, 1985.

18. The Upanishads.

19. The Vedas.